SOUL UNIVERSE
Create Your Dream Life

A Book From Lilyleaf11 Publishing Co.
Written By Indi B

ESTB 2021

PUBLISHING CO

"The Lotus flower is regarded in many different cultures, especially in eastern religions, as a symbol of purity, enlightenment, self-regeneration and rebirth. Its characteristics are a perfect analogy for the human condition: even when its roots are in the dirtiest waters, the Lotus produces the most beautiful flower."

"If you want to be perfect, just be yourself."

Lilyleaf11
PUBLISHING CO

CONTENTS

FOLLOW THE INSPIRATION

INTRODUCTION

When you look in the mirror, what do you see? What are you telling yourself? You are a seed ready to blossom. Your soul is on a creative journey. What is its purpose? When you go deep inside your soul, there is a knowing that there is so much more. Do you have any idea how truly amazing you really are? Discover how to unlock your soul's purpose and find true happiness.

I felt a need to write this book because I hear and see so many people just trying to get through life. Just trying to get through their day and are begging for the weekend to come or the next year to arrive. It just seems crazy that people haven't found true happiness in their lives.

I want people to feel good. So many of us don't realize our full potential and see how incredible we are. I have no idea if what I'm writing is true, but what is really true? We all have different truths. What one person believes is not the same as another's belief.

"You are always on your path; you don't have to get bogged down by others."

I feel like I didn't really write it. There was a knowing and a calling. A desire to put these words onto paper. It's a mash-up of things I've heard in podcasts, science programs, books, documentaries. It's things I've researched and studied along my journey.

I'm not saying you have to believe it. I would like you to come to your own conclusion. I would love for you to find more happiness in your life. If you can find your true essence, find what makes you feel good, then everything else will hopefully start to fall into place for you. Money, relationships, career. It can all flow much smoother than you think.

Life doesn't have to be hard. I don't believe it's supposed to be hard. It's a journey that should be enjoyed. Both the good and the bad.

Since I was young, I didn't really have a big belief in religion or what was out there. I kind of thought some of the peaceful religions would be more my style but I never really gravitated to any of them, and I started to think that there can't be a higher power or anything else out there because they wouldn't allow so much suffering to go on in the world. It also didn't feel right to me that so many people were so strict about how they had to live their lives.

Deep down, I could still feel there was something more. I loved yoga and would feel calm and a sense of wellness after doing sessions. We would do a few little meditations, then I'd notice I would get some inspiration and exciting ideas would come into my mind.

Then a few amazing people came into my life that started to explain that we are far more than we think we are. It was presented in a scientific way, through quantum physics and the quantum world.

Once I learned that we are cells, molecules, proteins, atoms and inside is energy, then it really made me want to dig deeper and find out more. Energy never dies. Where does this energy come from? Where did it begin? It must have come from somewhere. Yes, a big bang, but then how does the world sustain itself? Are we just a "miracle" that has never been repeated? Then I looked at the pyramids and the amazing things around the world that our ancestors have built which they struggle to recreate with the top equipment, engineering, and technology in this modern era. I said to myself, "I can't be so naive to think that it's just us in this entire universe."

The quantum world explains so much about what we are and how we got here.

When researching information from Space.com they discuss that for decades, science has said that humans are made of stardust.

"A new survey of 150,000 stars says that humans and their galaxy have about 97 percent of the same kind of atoms, and the elements of life appear to be more prevalent toward the galaxy's center, the research found.

"The crucial elements for life on Earth, often called the building blocks of life, can be abbreviated as CHNOPS: carbon, hydrogen, nitrogen, oxygen, phosphorus and sulfur. For the first time, astronomers have cataloged the abundance of these elements in a huge sample of stars" (Information from the website Space.com).

We are made of the same elements of stars, but that is just our physical body. What about our energetic body? The parts that are inside the atom.

As we know, through thermodynamics, energy cannot be created nor destroyed. It simply changes states. So where did the energy inside of us come from and where does it go?

Then I discovered the law of attraction. It's like gravity. It's there, but most of us don't really know how we are stuck upside down to a planet floating perfectly in space with a sun and a moon at the perfect proximity so we can all stick to the ground. So many of my words flow from the teachings of Abraham Hicks and I learned a lot from Dr Joe Dispenza. I'll talk about the quantum world and the law of attraction later in this book. It just shows why bad things happen to good people. We have total freedom here on earth to choose whoever we want to be. You can create any life you want. You just need to know how it works. It's time to stop putting limitations on what we can become.

I'm not saying there is more out there. This could be a complete coincidence that we ended up dangling upside down in the middle of space at the perfect speed between a sun and a moon. The earth formed beautifully with the right amount of water and sunlight. The plants grew to give us the exact amount of oxygen and there is no other being that exists out of the earth. It's up to you to decide.

I'm still figuring this all out. I will say my life is the best it's ever been and I'm the happiest I've ever been. I'm on a natural high. Stuff still goes on around me. People get sick or stressed and I still pay bills, but everything is easier. It doesn't bother me as much. Life is more exciting every day and I can be doing the most boring, mundane things if anyone else was observing me. It's so hard to explain until you actually get there. You do have to make time in the beginning to feel good. Then feeling good comes naturally and you realize you were exerting too much effort all along.

Keep reading and hopefully, you'll start to find tools to make you feel better. You don't want to live your life waiting for the weekend. Every day can feel like the weekend once you get to that stage of awareness.

It's always interested me that people and cultures have so many beliefs about life. Why has everyone got such a different viewpoint? Do we know what is real or what is a belief, or are beliefs real? I mean, you can definitely overthink everything. So many people refer to the soul, or they talk to loved ones that have passed on. They see angel numbers, feathers, or signs. Are we all just hallucinating, or is there something to it? There's a lot of research on the mind and body and how we are energetic beings. Where does the energy go? Does it stay with us?

Are we all energy? Are we consciousness creating this incredible world?

Everything in your life is what's going on in your energy field. Everything is being reflected back to you. You are more than your body. Can't you feel that there is something else within?

When slowing down, we have more time to listen and tune into the Universe. We give our bodies more healing time. We gain more knowledge and understanding. If we are going too fast and doing too much, then we miss the subtle sounds that the Universe is singing. We miss the breadcrumbs that guide us along our path and we can end up on the wrong track. By slowing down, we can become more abundant, more mindful, and have a greater awareness of our soul journey.

You are creating a new you. A more powerful, happier, aware you. A beautiful creator that has more knowledge, understanding and peace.

These are notes from my journeys. You can decide if you believe it or not. Some things may resonate now. Some might unfold later. Or some you may say, "This chick is crazy." It may seem a bit repetitive, but sometimes we need to hear things a few times for us to understand it.

Sometimes you may feel you have to search far and wide to find the meaning of life, but it can just be in your backyard.

This book is a beautiful, light reading for people feeling like they aren't reaching their full potential. That they can have more, work less, and feel pure happiness.

IT'S UP TO YOU TO HAVE FUN

APPRECIATE
LIFE   YOUR AMAZING

CHAPTER 1

WHO AM I?

"What lies behind you and what lies in front of you, pales in comparison to what lies inside of you"

- RALPH WALDO EMERSON.

Do you ever wonder where you really come from? That there is a deep knowing that there's something more? Some say there is a consciousness. A beautiful divine being that's energy is pure positivity and love. Total wellbeing. Some say that we all have this pure positive energy flowing through us. Still, sometimes we are so overwhelmed or distracted by what this amazing world has to offer that we lose our connection with it.

It's like changing the frequency and picking up a different radio station. It's still there, but you are not tuning into it. The higher your vibration, the closer you get to feeling good. So many people feel they have a soul, a guidance system, and intuition. Something they can feel and sense more than they can see.

Some say that in the center of the Universe, where it all began, there is beautiful energy full of light and unconditional love. It's where we came from and where we go back to. It's pure goodness, full of everything we love and desire. The Universe is vibrational. All of us can tap into the frequency of the Universe just like you tune into a radio station. You may have felt it before. The feeling of pure love, excitement, wellbeing, bliss. An all-knowing that everything is ok. A tingle. A vibe. A sense that there is something more. We are amazing beings. We get the opportunity to use all of our physical senses here on earth. We can touch, smell, taste, hear, see. Life is supposed to feel good. You didn't come here to watch others create. You came here for your own creations. You didn't come here to fix everything. You came here for the experience of life, showing you what you want—showing you what you can create and what you can become.

Some say that when we pass, we go back to that pure light and love energy. But be here in the now. Be in the present moment and turn dreams into the reality you want. Don't focus on what you don't have. Your thoughts are turning to things. You create your own reality. What vibration are you putting out there?

Are you programmed by society, cultures, teachers, and parents? Are you recreating your painstaking past? The more you let go of trying to control the past and the world around you, then the more you feel in control.

Follow the Good Feeling Thoughts

We are not here to be anxious, angry, frustrated, or depressed. We are soul beings here on earth to create and expand. These new ideas and dreams we come up with help the Universe evolve. It's ok to just enjoy life. We don't have to suffer because others are suffering. We are all souls finding our way. We chose to come back to this time to learn and create. All souls love one another. Some souls just forget who they are. From a human perspective, people have been misled, unsupported, and under-resourced. They have belief systems that make them think and act in a certain way. They would benefit from education, love, and guidance. Life is just about enjoying the little things. The keys are love, appreciation, happiness, and fun. If you can't do anything else, just start with satisfaction.

We have forgotten to see the beauty that is right in front of us. We are making life so complicated, feeling we have to have bigger and better and not stopping to see and appreciate how much we actually have. We have a head full of thoughts that don't even serve us.

I Interpret life as a journey we are lucky to go on. Earth is a place that offers our senses such delight. We have tastes, touch, smells, feelings. We have so many amazing opportunities to explore and discover. Our souls get to learn and move in different ways. We are not here to suffer, be sad, and worried. We get to feel those feelings, but we don't need to linger in them forever as they lower our own vibration. We get stuck in that vibrational consciousness.

"What you resist persists. Energy flows where attention goes."

I definitely don't have the qualifications to tell you where you came from. Still, I thought I'd share with you a few different perspectives I've been researching and learning on my journey. I'm not saying any of this is true. It's just what I have learned.

I would call myself a "modern hippie," someone who loves peace, love, and good vibes, but I also appreciate what contrast can bring to the table. If life was entirely perfect, we wouldn't grow, learn, evolve, create and reach our most incredible life. I became interested in quantum physics when I discovered energy only transforms. It doesn't actually get destroyed. It led me to the law of attraction and how we are all creating our own realities.

I have also been researching a lot of theories from scientists. The old science we were taught in school doesn't seem to add up anymore. People are getting injured or ill and stressed and have been dealing with health conditions. We are constantly repeating the same story, continuing to have the same limiting beliefs. We have told that story so many times that we have become that person—the person that is ill or the person that is stressed. It's time to tell a different story. One where we are happy, discovering how amazing we are and creating the life we desire. We can teach our nervous system to recalibrate and create the life we deserve.

Evolution?

We are evolving into our higher consciousness. So many new scientific discoveries have been discussed on how we are a complete species of our own. Our emotions and intelligence advanced so quickly all of a sudden. How did our DNA and chromosomes advance so complexly from the apes? Is this really who we evolved from?

DNA definition: "a self-replicating material that is present in nearly all living organisms as the main constituent of chromosomes. It is the carrier of genetic information."

Chromosome definition: "a threadlike structure of nucleic acids and protein found in the nucleus of most living cells, carrying genetic information in the form of genes." (Definitions from web page of Oxford Languages)

"The feeling that there's something more to our story is not just a recent phenomenon. Archaeological discoveries show that, almost universally, from the ancient Mayan and the indigenous traditions of the American desert Southwest to the roots of the world's major religions, ancient humans felt connected to more than just their immediate surroundings."

Gregg Braden describes that some "believe we have our roots in other worlds, some that we can't even see, and that we are ultimately part of a cosmic family that lives in those worlds."

His questions and research do make me wonder. "Could there be a simple explanation as to why such a sense has remained with us so strongly, across such diverse traditions, and has lasted for so long? Is it possible that our feeling of having an intentional origin and a greater potential is based on something that's true?" (From the official Gregg Braden website, Scientist, New York Times Best Seller, greggbraden.com)

Do we even belong in Darwin's evolutionary family? There have been a number of new theories that dismiss Darwin's theory.

Has our DNA been altered so we can become the intelligent, capable life forms that we are today? I have heard talk of divine architects creating our DNA. That would just prove how magical we really are. Some people believe that celestial guardians have implanted and upgraded our DNA. Is this why we are such a magnificent species? They come from different dimensional fields. That's why most of us don't see them. It's often said that different beings help create our world. A divine lineage has evolved over time. Some of us are from different stars. Some only incarnate every five hundred to one thousand years, some sooner, and some beings not at all. Those are what people would call angels and archangels and other "magical" beings—our guides and guardians. Some believe we reincarnate all of the time.

The reason we incarnate is to evolve and expand our consciousness, and this is done through the physical world. We are like the animal kingdom—all different, but fall under the same category. You can start to overthink it all. You can wonder where you truly came from. It's fun to dream, but we have to remember that life on this planet is such a treat. I don't think all planets are this amazing and offer so much contrast. You can believe what you want. I don't know if any of that is true, but there has been a lot of research lately on DNA.

I have read some interesting information from scientist Gregg Braden. He investigated studies from other scientists that used advanced techniques, with results that are accepted in the highest courts of law. The "scientists tested a Neanderthal infant's DNA to see how similar hers was to that of modern-day humans. Results showed we were not, in fact, descended from Neanderthals."

He explained that the "lack of common DNA between humans and less advanced primates all suggests that we may not belong on the same tree with the early hominids commonly shown in the textbooks."

"Evolution has occurred, but when it comes to us humans, it's a different story."

They are saying that the facts don't support the old theory of evolution of plants and animals and humans.

Gregg Braden goes on to say that "we appear to be a species of our own. Our DNA is a result of a rare arrangement of chromosomes, which are fused and optimized in a way that cannot be identified as random."

He's saying that our amazing emotions and feelings are very useful and they are more important than we previously thought.

"We're here with the bodies and the nervous systems that afford us the abilities of compassion, empathy, intuition, self-healing, and much more. The fact of their presence within us suggests that we're intended to utilize—and master—the sensitivities that we arrived with."

Information is from the official Gregg Braden website Gregg Braden - Bridging Science, Spirituality & the Real World (greggbraden.com 2021)

Spiritual Hoarder

I have done a few meditation workshops & Zoom meditations with a Guru who learned how to connect with the Universe in a cave with his "Master" in the Himalayas. Now that's the real deal. He definitely brings you up a level of vibration with his powerful words and connection. He laughs and tells us we are lucky we don't have to go and live in a cave to become enlightened. People often think they have to travel to the ends of the earth to find themselves, but we can easily do it on the couch at home.

He would call me a "Spiritual Hoarder," someone who does a bit of everything. He didn't say it literally to me. Still, he talked about it over Zoom one night to a group of us, and I actually liked that analogy. I'm happy just being me and doing what I feel comfortable with. I love to embrace everyone and find people have a bit of their own flavor that I can add to my mix. I find inspiration in others. I think everyone in this world has so much to offer. Just because we might not understand someone doesn't mean they are wrong. Most people do the things they do because that's what they've been taught. Instead of judging each other, it would be amazing to see where they're coming from. Everyone has their own opinions and beliefs, and that's ok. Some days, I don't want to believe in anything at all, and that's fine as well. Some days, I think I must be crazy to believe there's more out there. I was told we can't be so naive to believe that the world is in perfect alignment with the sun and the moon on the perfect axis with exactly the same distance to both and the exact amount of oxygen that we need is provided for us to breathe every day.

"We would like you to reach the place where you're not willing to listen to people criticize one another… where it matters to you so much that you feel good, that you are only willing to think positive things about people… you are willing to look for positive aspects; you are only willing to look for solutions, and you are not willing to beat the drum of all the problems of the world." - Abraham Hicks

I like to believe that we have guidance and support from what we would call "the other side." Some call it heaven. You can call it whatever you like.

There are so many mixed ideas and beliefs but that's ok. I just love finding what resonates with me. It's great to start fresh and think about the belief systems you have. Did they come from you, or did they come from parents, teachers, friends, or other areas?

I like to really focus on myself first. Connect with my heart and feel the goodness that surrounds me.

They didn't just plonk all the losers on Earth. We haven't come here to prove anything to anyone. We have come for expansion, for evolution. To see what we can be. People think they have to prove their worth. We do not realize just how powerful we really are. We are super creators.

There's a field of energy that connects all things. But where did it begin?

The meaning of "Source" as defined in (dictionary.com) is "A place, person or thing from which something originates."

I've heard of Source energy being described as pure, positive energy. Can you feel wellbeing? The call of the Universal energy feels like joy, love and, appreciation. It feels like liquid love. It ripples through your body. It wants you to create, be inspired. It wants you to learn, grow, develop, and evolve.

The Universe Sees You As Worthy

Do you think you need to try harder to get further ahead? Well, you don't. Try less and see what happens. When you try less, things seem to flow and fall into place so much easier. Just start by feeling satisfied where you are.

The Universe sees you as so worthy and so amazing. I promise you didn't get sent here to prove your worth. You could not be more deserving to get what you want. Don't feel guilty or unworthy. Don't feel that it's not fair if you get things and others don't. Any one of us can have whatever we want. We all have our own journey. You don't have to fix everyone.

Everything around us and inside of us are atoms. Inside is energy. Energy oscillates so essentially it's a vibration. When I discuss vibes or vibration, I'm referring to all objects because everything in us, on this planet, and in this Universe is energy, so every single thing vibrates with its own speed and rhythm. It's kind of like musical instruments playing a different beat or at a different pace.

Sometimes when we have heavier, denser energy, for example, we are feeling tired or stuck or we are feeling a lack of abundance, we are like a weight being pulled down by the earth. The law of gravity is pulling harder to keep us on the earth, so we don't float away. So when you're feeling good, you're feeling lighter, you've cleared out all the unwanted blocks in your body. The emotional blocks are just thicker, stuck energy. So once they've gone, you weigh less energetically. It's like a balloon. Say it's been held down with a weight. It's a heavier weight, so the balloon is stuck to the ground. When you clear out your unwanted energetic baggage, you release the weight and feel lighter, like you're floating. I'm not saying you're going to float off into the sunset, but once you really start to feel good, you do feel like you're a lot lighter.

CHAPTER 2

SOUL CONNECTION

"The oneness of the Universe is Love."

- RAM DASS

Soul Journey, what is your soul calling for? I watched an interesting program with Matias De Stefano (Gaia.com). He feels he can remember things that have happened in the past. The Universe started with nothingness. A void. Something that you can't explain because there's nothing. I know it's frustrating to think about what was there before nothing, but you could go crazy trying to work out nothing. I'm sure there's someone that can explain it better than me. Maybe after we transition, it will all become clearer. I've had the beginning of time explained to me in a few different ways. I can't say what is the truth.

Matias explains that out of the nothingness came a beautiful energy. A being, a creator, a life force, something that is pure positive energy. An incredible soul or being—pretty much there are no words to describe the eternal magical vibe that comes from the source of the Universe. The Source means the beginning, where it all began. This beautiful energy wanted to know who it was, so it said, "I am," and so it began.

The waves of its thinking echoed through the Universe. The waves of thinking are a vibration. Each thought has a different vibration, meaning it has a different frequency. A new thought created a new dream. Each dream expanded like the roots of a tree. Each thought is like a seed. Each seed grows into a tree. More thoughts, more vibration, more expansion. This went on for a very long time. No one can say because there was no time.

This amazing consciousness continued to ask, "Who am I?" until one day the number of vibrations and frequencies and pure light created a huge bang—the big bang theory. Then this is where the energy became more solid. The denser the energy, the more "matter" there is.

After that, the dreams & creations of beings kept continuing and slowly, over time, different atoms created planets, cells, and other extraordinary things. (Inside of atoms is pure energy.)

The definition of matter is "physical substance in general, as distinct from mind and spirit; (in physics) that which occupies space and possesses rest mass, especially as distinct from energy." - Oxford Dictionary

So after the big bang, solid objects were formed and turned to matter. But inside all matter still lies the energy.

If we all originally came from the same place, is that like a bloodline, but instead, we all have the same energy flowing through us?

You are so much more incredible and powerful than you know. Don't let your thoughts control you. We are making our lives way too complicated. Life is about having fun. Feeling good should be your success. It's not about how much you do, where you've been, or what status you have. It's just about enjoying life. You are always on your path, but sometimes you can just move off it slightly. That's why you can feel negative emotions. It's your "inner being," "soul," or whatever you want to call it, not agreeing with you. The Universe wants you to enjoy what you have. Don't look at your life as having a "lack of." Look at your life and appreciate what you have. If you are full of abundance, then you will have more and more.

The vibration/ frequency you put out into the world is what you'll get back. If you are feeling angry, you will attract angry people. If you're feeling anxious, you'll attract anxious people. Notice how you're feeling. Every day, focus on trying to turn your thoughts into positive ones. If you can't stop thinking about something negative, then just change the subject. Every day gets easier and better. Soon it becomes normal to wake up happier. Your intuition will start to tell you what you need and bring you all you ask for. Just "get happy"!

You are a magnet for the way you feel. Don't attract what you don't want. Focus on happiness and draw that into your life.

You can't control the conditions, but you can control how you feel. Focus on what brings love, goodness, and color into your day. The more negativity you focus on, the more you bring into your life. If you notice others are angry, frustrated or do you wrong, then just remember maybe they need a bit of extra love in their lives. Perhaps they've lost themselves. Those people need support and encouragement to find their way home. Focus on the good that surrounds you. Find things in your life that you appreciate. There has been a bit of talk about how you can create your own reality and the law of attraction. It's said that the law brings you things depending on how you feel, not always something that you want. The law of attraction is always fair but not always even. If you are complaining about everything around you, then you are just drawing more of that energy into your life. Focus on the little moments that feel good, and you'll find you attract more good feeling thoughts.

Your thoughts matter a lot. The reason they matter is that your thoughts are the reason for the way you feel.

There has been a lot of talk lately saying that we are a unit of consciousness. You can tap into that consciousness and get any information you like. You can even get other people's thoughts and information, so that's why you need to look after yourself and feel stronger, so you don't let all the random thoughts come in from all over the place. That energy of someone else's thoughts or your thoughts never disappears because energy doesn't die, so it's out there floating around. It was explained to me once that it's like an iCloud. It sounds insane but why doesn't an iCloud or storage from a device sound weird? It's all energy, so it's all the same thing.

The Universe is one big server with all our thoughts, feelings, energy, and vibrations floating around in it. It's good to be aware of the energy you are putting out there. If you're at a concert and everyone's having a great time, you're in the zone. The energy lifts you and makes you feel high. If you're in a crowd with everyone protesting, then everyone starts fighting and the momentum builds, and you can't stop. That energy is going out there into the Universe. That's why even starting with putting out good energy from yourself can help the whole of the Universe. I know what energy I would rather put out there.

If I'm fighting against everyone and everything, then that's the same energy as a crowd full of protestors. You can achieve so much more if you are putting out positive energy. If you are fighting against things, then the problem only becomes more prominent. Solutions are so much better than problems. Which one would you rather focus on? Problems or solutions? It's ok, though, because solutions still come out of problems and the people who make them.

Scientists say that harmonizing the heart and brain can lead to anti-aging. Brain and heart coherence are very valuable. Your heart does not just pump blood around your body.

We have extraordinary abilities. We just need to awaken these potentials. That goosebump feeling you get shows that you are in alignment with your soul. It's a little tingle from the Universal energy surging through your body. If you're always thinking about pros and cons, then you lose momentum on the positives.

Some say there's a beautiful world beyond our world. A world where all of our dreams have been manifested. A world where we let go of the struggle, the resistance, and the pain. The feeling of pure bliss flows through you. You are total positive energy. This world is indescribable to man. The colors, the sensations, the pleasure is far more than anyone can imagine. Everything you have been creating over lifetimes is in this realm. The best of the best. The things you most love, cherish and aspire to be.

Every time we put something in motion on earth, we get another step closer to creating our dream world. The contrast helps us know what we like and what we don't like. When we eventually transition back to this incredible realm. We have everything we want and beyond.

On this physical earth, we cannot forget what a privilege it is to be here. Can you imagine being in a totally blissful world? It would be amazing, but do expansion and evolution happen as fast? Do we get to create, learn and grow as much?

What I love about Earth is its beauty. We get to experience this fantastic planet. It's beyond incredible with all of its wonders. I've heard it described as each area having its own personality. Every beach, every mountain, every river, every lake. They all have their own uniqueness.

It is said that we are creators. Before we came to earth, we were truly remarkable in every way. We are still those incredible beings, but we have lost sight of just how amazing we are.

The "real world" on Earth has taught us in some ways that we need to struggle; we need to prove ourselves. We need to work hard. Centuries and centuries of humans telling us all of these mixed messages, and we have forgotten just how much power, strength, and beauty we have.

The kids that come into this world know it, but we start to tell them otherwise. We say, "Life is hard. You have to work hard. Be careful. Don't do that. Parents know better." It goes on and on until eventually these children, including ourselves, have submitted to believing that it's normal to struggle.

Energy Drainers

If you're connected to the energy of the Universe, then no one should be able to drain your energy.

I like to visualize a bubble or sphere or swirling light full of strong, powerful energy flowing around me daily. It's protection against everything you think might come your way. Humans, electromagnetic rays, media. Whatever you're feeling is zapping your energy. I try not to overthink everything as well. If you're thinking someone is going to drain your energy, then it's more likely they will. You're way more powerful than you think you are so there's no need for anyone or anything to interfere with your space.

You just need to keep yourself connected. Find higher frequencies, vibrations, things that make you feel good. The higher your vibration the higher you are from the negative energy suckers. If you're feeling good, no one can take you down. They just pass you by.

I talk more about the law of attraction in other chapters but pretty much I liken it to a magnet. Visualize a magnetic field or if it's easier, just visualize a small magnet. The magnet is your emotions. You are pulling in with the magnet the same emotions that you are feeling. That's why people get stuck, or they repeat old habits. That's why history repeats itself.

If you're feeling angry your magnet or magnetic field is pulling in people around you that are angry. So you're noticing everyone is angry. So you are telling yourself, "Look, see I'm right. Everyone is angry."

If you are feeling appreciation, then the magnet or magnetic field is pulling you towards people that are appreciating life. It's the same for any feeling you have.

Chakra Energy Points

In Sanskrit, the word "chakra" means "disk" or "wheel" and refers to the energy centers in your body. These wheels or disks of spinning energy each correspond to certain nerve bundles and major organs.

Who knows how many chakras we actually have? Some say 114 but some say way more. Apparently, there are *seven* main chakras that people can agree on.

Some believe that if your energy system is out of balance, this can mean your emotions are out of balance, which can lead to physical disease and illness. You can find examples online of different illnesses relating to chakra blockages. If you have an illness or a physical ailment, your chakra system may not be flowing as well as you would like. Please don't overthink it as well. The more you start to think something is wrong the more momentum you put on it.

The main chakras people often start with are:

Root chakra - Muladhara is located at the base of your spine. It provides you with your foundation and can help you feel grounded. It's responsible for your security and stability.

Sacral chakra - Svadhisthana is located just below your navel. This chakra is responsible for your sexual and creative energy. It's also linked to how you relate to your emotions as well as the emotions of others.

Solar plexus chakra - Manipura is located in your stomach area. It's responsible for confidence and self-esteem, as well as helping you feel in control of your life.

Heart chakra - Anahata is located near your heart, in the center of your chest. The heart chakra is all about our ability to love and show compassion.

Throat chakra - Vishuddha is located in your throat. This chakra has to do with our ability to verbally communicate.

Third eye chakra - Ajna is located between your eyes. You can thank this chakra for a strong gut instinct. That's because the third eye is responsible for intuition. It's also linked to imagination.

Crown chakra - Sahasrara is located at the top of your head. Your Sahasrara represents your spiritual connection to yourself, others, and the universe.

There are so many ways to balance your chakras. You just have to find what resonates with you.

(Chakra Information inspired by articles in Healthline.com)

The Energy

Although it may sound far-fetched to most humans, energy is the universal language of all living things. Whether you're a dog, a human, a bird, or a plant, everything is powered by energy. I'll define energy as I see it and then explain its relationship to, and therapeutic effect on, your life. As previously said, energy is the universal language of all life. How does it operate, then?

Everything at the molecular level is composed of free-floating energy particles. Combining this energy determines whether one bundle of energy becomes a fish or a human, for example. Regardless of its arrangement, energy remains the same at its fundamental level and is naturally free-floating. This signifies that it is transferable and shareable. Of course, not on a visible level, but we can surely feel it. For instance, have you ever had the sensation that the phone was about to ring or met someone who gave you a positive/negative vibe? That is energy in action! This is not some mythical force; rather, it is the "free-floating" energy that moves through the world on a subatomic level and is picked up by our natural "receptor" as feelings or "sixth senses." Now, as humans who acted on these principles previously, we have evolved significantly and established language as our primary mode of communication.

Energetic blocks are frequently the result of emotional upheavals, such as fear or shock. An effective technique to resolve any issues in life is through energy healing. If energy is the source of the problem, it is also the source of the solution.

If you lack a degree in quantum physics, have no fear. Here is an explanation of the concepts with which science and spirituality are wrestling.

Everything is made out of energy. It's all about atoms and subatomic particles and possibly even smaller particles or what they are now saying are energy waves.

Subatomic particles/ waves can act as matter particles—extremely small particles zipping around—or as flowing energy waves.

Many of us feel that something exists outside the material universe (what our biological minds can see right now). This could be referred to as a quantum field or another dimension. Whatever name is given to it, it is a realm of greater vibrations containing solely pure energy.

There is no distinction between pure and matter-energy; energy flows.

It appears that the process by which energy takes on the material form is inextricably related to some consciousness. Quantum physicists have revealed that without the involvement of a conscious mind, no matter could be formed.

When energy transforms into matter or takes on form, it becomes a distinct intelligence. The atoms that comprise an eye are identical to those that comprise my table, but each has unique information.

Emotions, biological structures, energetic structures, thoughts, and energy or information passing through our field all affect the human energy field. (These are the fundamental influencing elements.)

Emotions are "directed energy," which is another way of saying they are a highly directed flow of information. Emotions communicate with our biological structures. Tissues, organs, and systems carry out this "direction." However, it is a two-way street, and if tissues or organs contain misdirected energy, it might influence us emotionally.

What does this signify for energy healing practitioners? To put it one way, when organized energy gets disorganized, they can encounter difficulties. How does energy degrade into disorganization? Does energy become distorted when it is changed from its natural conditions?

Each of us can hold extraordinary amounts of information or energy. We evolve by increasing our capacity to hold higher and higher vibrational information. As a result, if the distortion in our energy is severe enough, we will feel it. And if these distortions take us away from what our energy intelligence or soul is supposed to carry, we feel it intensely. These "distortions" may result from us holding an energy frequency that is too low for us (we may be locked in an old pattern or fearful of holding a higher vibration), necessitating the need to raise our vibration.

Have I lost you yet? When I first started learning this, I was slightly overwhelmed and super excited at the same time. I just kept going and the more I heard, the more it all started to make sense. Don't worry if it doesn't make sense now. It will in the future.

What causes our energy to become distorted or disorganized and how can you assist it in shifting and clearing back into a state of balance and clarity, into a higher form that is more aligned with your own unique soul needs? This can be accomplished by supporting the overall energetic structure of the human energy field (which is self-aware) or by addressing any of the elements affecting this field. Additionally, we can assist the energetic system by connecting to the universal energy field and even this enigmatic "other," which has pure energy knowledge, to bring in clear energetic structures and energy/information to aid in the process.

Energy work is about reorganizing energy to flow freely, and the knowledge carried is as pure as possible for each of us on our evolutionary path. And because energy can shift and alter in response to our thoughts, whether mine or yours, as well as its inherent intelligence, energy healing has the potential to shift and modify our personal experience and physical health. I do believe we can heal ourselves and we don't need anyone else but it's always fun to get extra help and guidance on the way.

Energy Medicine

Energy medicine is an umbrella word that refers to several complementary and alternative healing approaches. While many of these therapies have gained prominence in recent years, the majority have their origins in the world's earliest medical systems and early spiritual traditions. As with its historical forerunners, these therapies begin with the premise that subtle energies surround and permeate everything in the universe.

Current energy medicine practitioners are focused on the unseen vital energy, or life force believed to circulate throughout the body. This energy, variously referred to as qi, ki, and prana affects a person's health. According to energy medicine practitioners, the movement of energy within a person forms a perceptible "biofield."

Certain energy healers can detect temperature fluctuations associated with certain parts of the body. Other energy healers perceive the presence of an aura around the body. Others intuitively perceive oscillations in the biofield. In any event, when the internal flow of vital energy is unobstructed and balanced, the biofield is considered to be harmonious, and health is at its peak. Alternatively, a disturbance or disruption in a person's biofield suggests the presence of a medical or psychological condition conducive to sickness.

Energy healers attempt to communicate directly with a client's biofield during therapy sessions. Their objective is twofold: to detect biofield disruptions and to rebalance the energy flow within the individual. Numerous complementary and alternative therapies are based on the fundamental concepts of energy medicine. Acupuncture, for example, is founded on the concept that the human body contains recognizable energy pathways called meridians. However, those therapeutic techniques that are fully non-invasive are of particular interest. The energy healer sends healing energy to enhance the client's vital energy in these ways. The additional energy offered by the healer assists in unblocking the client's energy flow and enables the client's internal healing processes to operate more efficiently.

Energy work, or energy healing, as I define it, is the act of reorganizing energy or energetic information. Energy and information are inextricably linked. Energy is data. It possesses consciousness or intellect. And by examining the energy of objects, we might gain insight into what we are seeing or feeling.

Reiki, Therapeutic Touch, and Healing Touch are three common non-invasive modalities of energy healing. But there are so many more that I would need to investigate further. (BodyTalk, Kinesiology, Aura Cleansing, Somatic Experience, Tapping, Polarity Balancing, Chakra Balancing, Sound Healing, and the list goes on.)

Reiki - Reiki is a type of energy healing that originated in late nineteenth-century Japan. In this approach, the practitioner acts as a conduit for the client to receive a universal life force. The practitioner distributes this energy to the client through a specialized sort of "laying on of hands." Typically, the practitioner works through a pre-defined sequence of hand movements from head to foot. Generally, training to become a Reiki healer entails a series of attunements that enable the healer to connect to the Universe's life force. (I would thoroughly check out anyone attempting to do this for you. It's important to have someone with experience, positivity, and the right advice)

Therapeutic Touch - Therapeutic Touch is comparable to Reiki in many aspects but was established in the 1970s within the American nursing tradition. The practitioner works with the patient's biofield from a few inches above. The practitioner investigates the biofield for obstructions and constrictions using lengthy, deliberate hand strokes. When such obstructions are found, the practitioner attempts to smooth them down and restore the free flow of energy. Therapeutic Touch is currently taught in a growing number of nursing schools worldwide.

Healing Touch - Healing Touch is a 1980s version of Therapeutic Touch. Healing Touch balances and clears the biofield through the use of both light and near touch. Again, the goal is to facilitate the body's natural ability to heal by ensuring an unobstructed flow of vital energy throughout the individual. The American Holistic Nurses Association has sanctioned both Healing Touch and Therapeutic Touch. Healing Touch is now incorporated into the patient care systems of over twenty-five institutions in the United States.

Other Forms of Energy Healing

Energy meditation is a technique for channeling the Universe's energy into your own body for attunement and wellness. There are various types of energies, including Reiki and Mahatma. Meditation is an ancient technique that is supposed to assist in relieving stress and anxiety, promoting a sense of peace, and even promoting longevity.

According to energy meditation principles, persons have "auras" surrounding them that are energy centers called "chakras." Certain individuals are thought to be able to see chakras. Additionally, there are methods for photographing them. Each energy has a unique frequency, and meditating enables one to become more conscious of their own.

Because chakra energies are at various levels, it takes time and determination to get to them, yet they have the potential to develop spiritual awareness and consciousness. Everything in our environment is made up of energy. Inner serenity is achieved through meditating on this. Anyone can meditate in the comfort of their own homes. All that is required is a quiet place and some free time.

The meditator then concentrates on a mantra, a sound, a spoken phrase, an item, an image, or anything else they desire to focus on. It requires practice and patience. While sitting silently for twenty minutes is difficult, with experience, it is possible. The meditator emerges from the meditation rested, rejuvenated, and revitalized.

Spreading positive and kind thoughts throughout the world is another part of energy meditation. When we reflect on these things, we gain a greater understanding of the broad picture and where we need to be in our lives, as well as the steps necessary to get there. Meditation can assist in relaxing and relieving concerns, nerves, and tensions, as well as assisting in relieving health problems. Meditation practices can act as a guiding factor, assisting people in finding serenity in their world.

Pranic Healing: This type of healing is all about channeling the body's life force to heal the body's energy. This therapy is focused on the energy of a person's body or aura. In this therapy, energy is employed to cleanse the body of toxins, hence expediting the physical healing process.

Crystal Healing: In this healing technique, stones and crystals extract pollutants from the body. These stones and crystals have varying effects on the body and address various physical, emotional, and energetic issues. They deflect "negative" energy from the body, which can wreak havoc on your energetic, mental and physical health.

Quantum Healing: This is a form of healing that is based on the notion of resonance. Through breathing and visualization of energy flow, the body's energy level is increased. Quantum Healing is a practice that also has beneficial effects on the immune system. Quantum techniques use the body's energy system to determine why a person is experiencing a symptom, an illness, or a "behavioral" problem. Energetic disturbances are at the root of the problem, both physical and nonphysical.

Qigong Therapy: This is used to restore the body's balance. With a four-thousand-year history, Qigong combines synchronized body movements, breathing, and meditation to promote health and spirituality. The therapy originated in Chinese medicine and is thought to balance the body's positive energy, necessary for wellness.

Feng Shui: The Chinese words "Feng" and "Shui" translate to mean "wind" and "water." This concept is derived from an ancient poem about human life being connected and flowing with the environment around it.

The philosophy of Feng Shui is a practice of arranging the pieces in living spaces in order to create balance with the natural world. The goal is to harness energy forces and establish harmony between an individual and their environment. Feng Shui teaches us how to achieve peace with our environment.

Ayurveda: This is aimed at harnessing the mind-body relationship to heal and promote longevity. It's one of the world's oldest holistic healing systems. The term originates from *Sanskrit*.

In Ayurvedic texts, Dosha balance is emphasized. It is described that we have three elemental doshas—Vata, Pitta, and Kapha. We can be a balance of one or all doshas. Ayurveda is used to promote harmony with the Universe.

Have you heard of people talk about an "aura"? This can be interpreted differently in many parts of the world. Science tells us that as human beings we radiate electricity that's also known as an electromagnetic field. Healthline.com describes an aura as "the 'energy' someone around you omits." Some people make you nervous—others relax you. Your energy may tell someone around you if you're angry, sad, anxious, or excited.

Each layer of your aura is said to have a different color. The colors can change over time. This is dependent on how you're feeling, and what's going on in your life.

An excerpt from mindbodygreen.com explains that, "Aura's are thought of as the unseen energy field surrounding a person's physical body. The aura's can be affected by someone's physical and emotional state."

Energy healing has increased in popularity over the last few years. Simultaneously, several anecdotal reports and small-scale studies have demonstrated the efficacy of energy healing in reducing anxiety, relieving pain, and expediting healing. However, because scientific measurement of the human biofield has only recently been proven, energy therapy applications continue to be controversial among traditionally trained physicians. I think the change is in the air though because there are some amazing physicians and scientists that are incorporating a holistic health approach where they are looking at all aspects of your being. More equipment is being developed that is starting to measure more in this area.

It is said that the healer holds the space and allows the well-being to flow through someone. I have also been told that connective tissue is said to hold your memories. Sometimes we may need to release the negative memories out of the body.

There are so many amazing people out there that can help you get started. If you're one of those people that really needs a bit of extra support and fine tuning, then find someone that resonates with you. Julia from

Elevate Health has taught me a lot. She has learned a technique called "BodyTalk" and helps people to get in tune with their own healing and guidance system.

"As a certified BodyTalk Practitioner I help to remove stuck emotions and belief systems/hard wired programming that is no longer serving you. Using cutting edge, non-evasive, Quantum Physics methods, I assist people in freeing their energy centers and connect you back to source. Everything is energy and life is about flow and balance. People come to me with anxiety, debilitating aches and pains, serious illness and totally fatigued. After a few sessions, they have cleared blockages and reset their ability to self heal." Julia Prescott

You just need to find what resonates with you. Like I've said before, the person must feel right. I've heard of people doing reiki sessions on others and the energy they are emitting is not that positive. They could be really frustrated and stressed out themselves. You want someone that is working with energy to have a calmer, more peaceful vibe. I think that's what attracted me to Julia—her welcoming, calming, positive presence. Someone that's completely stressed out would not be my pick to help me bring in healing and clarity.

What do you think would happen if you're feeling worried? You get a lot of worried people that come into your life. You get podcasts and tv shows and the news that says everyone is worried, so that becomes your reality, and you get stuck in a vicious cycle going around and around. The thoughts of being worried build momentum and you just get more and more worrying thoughts. The magnet is powerful. It's bringing you what you are attracting. It's not the magnet's fault. It's not your fault. You have the freedom to choose to be worried. The Universe says it's ok to worry. It knows, in the end, you are going to be fine. You are learning through your worry and becoming a stronger, more resilient being. You are creating more wants, dreams and desires for your best life.

But wouldn't it be lovely if you could get to your best life without having to go through so much of the worry and stress? Do you want to break free and make life more enjoyable and relaxed? You can still learn, grow, and evolve by having fun.

Stop focusing on the worry and slowly every day try to find a subject that feels better. The law of attraction will start to bring you more of this.

If a feeling of money feels better you can focus on having it but sometimes it's such a big subject to start with. It has so much resistance on it already. It's good to practice with easier subjects first. Focus on manifesting or drawing in little things with your magnet.

The basic thing that made me feel good was butterflies. I just focused on them, and they started to fly into my life in different ways. Butterflies probably seem boring to most people, but I would start off with something basic.

See what you can attract. If you want to attract good things with your magnet, then you need to stop focusing on the negative things. Don't try to stop thinking about the negatives, just focus on a completely different subject. Simple things like how the water feels on your face in the shower. It's completely basic stuff. Don't overthink it. The more you try and find something good to focus on the harder it gets. It's best if you're struggling just to try to live in the present moment, be satisfied and practice your mindfulness skills.

Like I have said before, life is never perfect in our eyes. Contrast still happens. Things go wrong. People get sick. We can suffer and get overwhelmed for everyone else and ourselves or we can reset each day and start again. Don't you find that if one thing goes wrong then everything starts to go wrong? "Things come in threes." Is that the magnet bringing in more of this? If you can turn the magnet in another direction towards something that feels better, then do that.

You can't heal your sore leg if you're saying it's never going to heal. Well, you can but it will take much longer. It's not going to get better if you keep telling yourself you probably need surgery or it's never going to be the same. Your body rejuvenates itself all the time. The cells repair daily. Why are you telling your cells that they can't repair themselves?

Cell Repair

One of the most amazing aspects of the human body is its ability to heal itself. There are thirty to forty trillion cells in the human body. These cells work tirelessly to achieve equilibrium. Every day they are trying to get us back to a natural balance.

When we abuse our bodies, or we are not looking after ourselves we can tell our cells the opposite things to help heal. They can be damaged or destroyed, sometimes in large quantities. However, these cells have the ability to heal or replace themselves. These all work to keep the body functioning at optimal levels.

All of the cells in our body regenerate at different times. Our liver can regenerate, our heart, our bones. Every single cell is energy, and they all repair themselves. But can you imagine these poor little cells when we are stressed, angry and frustrated? We are telling our cells you are sick; you are ill, you are tired. You can't repair yourself. Imagine the mixed messages.

They are programmed to heal. But you are confusing them by all of the contrast. It's not your fault. Life gets in the way. We haven't been taught enough about how cells replicate and multiply and regenerate. Well some of us have but we didn't really take it in. Some of us know that cells repair nonstop, but we don't really think about how what we are doing affects them.

You can heal your whole entire body so quickly. You may have injured your shoulder ten years ago, but you should have a whole new shoulder by now. Your cells should have regenerated, but it depends on what you are teaching them. If you're saying, "My shoulder still hurts. I have an injured shoulder. I hurt my shoulder years ago. I can't do that because I hurt my shoulder. No one understands that my shoulder is sore." What are you telling the new cells that are being created?

The old cells will keep telling the new cells that you have an injury. The same with illness or disease or other ailments. If your story is that you have always had eczema, or a sore knee, or you've always got a headache, don't you think the new cells are going to be programmed by the old cells to believe that this is the way you are? This person has all of these things going on so let's keep that in motion.

Don't you want to tell a different story? Tell one where you feel good. You are healthy. Your skin looks good. You feel young and full of energy. I know this is hard when you're feeling like crap but just try to change your unconscious thought patterns day by day.

Listen to what you are saying. At the end of the day reflect back. What was I telling myself? What did I tell that person in the street and at the supermarket? At the gym did I say I struggle? Or did I say I did a bit better than last week? Did I say my knee hurts, or did I say sometimes it feels a bit better? Listen to what you are telling the world. Is that the story you want to put out there?

If you have anxiety try not to tell yourself you have anxiety. Try to find better feeling thoughts. Remember the magnet will only bring you more anxiety and more people with anxiety and more energies leftover from other anxious people.

To rid your anxiety, you need to slowly move up the emotional scale. Check out the Abraham Hicks Emotional scale when you get a chance. It's on abrahamhicks.com or search for it on Pinterest. You'll see the emotions go up each level to finally feel really good. You can't just jump up to the top from feeling sick, unhappy, anxious, and fearful straight away, but if you keep practicing all of a sudden it all falls into place and each day you start to feel better than you used to. Sometimes you fall back into the old patterns and behaviors, but you find you notice and recognize that familiar feeling and it doesn't feel so good, so you bring yourself back up faster into better feeling thoughts.

It took me a while at the start. I got a bit frustrated with myself for not doing a perfect job and being amazingly happy every day. It's a process and takes practice. You still have days where contrast hits and something has gone wrong, but you ask yourself why it went wrong without overthinking it. You realize your emotions are feeling a bit down, so you find simple things to bring you back up. You can have a range of emotions all at once.

I've done a few workshops on releasing blocks which can cause illness, injuries, and other ailments. It amazed me how many people felt like they weren't worthy. They weren't worthy of love. They weren't worthy of money and a good job. I just couldn't believe so many people felt that way. We are all worthy no matter who we are and where we come from. Whatever your beginnings you are completely worthy.

We have to release what we have been told and what has been role modeled for us. A teacher, parents, friends could have made us feel unworthy or even our mind could have tricked us to think we are unworthy. You have no idea how incredible you truly are. You still have the energy from the source of the Universe. Everything and everyone has organically come from the source so that energy still flows through all of us. It's like having royal blood. Instead, conscientiousness doesn't have blood, so it's energy.

We are all connected. "Quantum Entanglement". We are all equally worthy. It doesn't matter where you've been, what you've done and how much you own. We all have that power inside of us that has been here since before the beginning of time. You have to realize how completely incredible you are. You're not just some random on-the-side creation. You are part of the pure life force creation. It flows through every cell in your body. It's time to remember how astounding you are. You are ready to flourish. Take control of your mind, body and soul and get back to who you are. Don't let beliefs or society's opinions control you. They have no power over you. They only have power if you let them.

Play fun visualizing or manifesting games like the car park game. Have a deep knowing that you're going to get a great car parking spot. Focus on attracting something easy like a butterfly. It might not be in the sky; it might be a butterfly picture. Have a knowing you're going to find a feather. Start off with fun things and see what happens. When you start to bring yourself up the emotional scale, you'll find others around you playing the same games.

Angel Numbers? 11:11

There's been a lot of talk about angel numbers and signs. I think these are amazing. You can create your own book of codes. You can interpret or perceive anything you want.

Whatever you're focusing on and however you're feeling you are going to draw that in. So, if you're focusing on negative folklore, you are more likely to bring in things with that same vibration. The law of attraction brings you what you're thinking about. If you want more comforting, guiding, loving energy then focus on that. I've heard that we as humans interpret angels or energies as we want to imagine it. If we want them to look like angels they do. If we want them to look like ghosts they do. If we want them to look like orbs they do. It's your perception. There's no right or wrong. It's up to you what you want to believe.

I remember getting so excited when I would see 11:11. A popular "Angel" number. I think you can start to create your own way of interpreting energy.

When interpreting signs and symbols, you can write a list of what you would like them to mean. For example, "I want 888 to mean more money is coming." 11:11 is, "I am guided and protected." You can make up whatever you like but I feel it's good to write it down then kind of stick to that; otherwise, it gets a bit confusing. You can add to it and tweak it. It's your own "guidance download." Guidance from your inner being, angels, Source, guidance system—whatever you like to call it.

When you think about it, the other side is not scary. All of our movies, folklore, some religions and stories have made things seem scary, so we have put those thoughts out there and they are there forever now, so we created those negative energies about things. But once we pass, I feel all of the negative energies, resistance and beliefs all fall away and we are back to pure positive energy.

If we pass over to the other side, we are not just going to say see you later to everyone and everything we have done on earth. We want to be here, check it out. See what people and loved ones are up to. This is why there are so many crazy ghost stories. But remember if you do focus on the negative energies made up by humans then you can still draw that in, and the law of attraction will bring you more.

It's hard to describe. It's not real, but we have made it real by so many people focusing on it. A collective consciousness of thoughts. Movies and books have had a big role to play.

I would just continue to focus on good energies.

I've heard people say that when we pass, there are still people fighting for justice, but that could be the energies that found it all interesting still coming back to see what we are up to. I've heard it said that when we pass, we don't just sit around listening to or playing the harp and relaxing.

It's exciting to come back and continue where you left off. So if you were fighting for justice here on earth then in the afterlife you're going to pop in or across or through the veil and see what everyone's up to. I will definitely be coming back to see what everyone is doing. I've been told that when we pass it's just like walking through a door. We don't need to be scared or worried. It's pure positive bliss.

Don't you find yourself talking to loved ones that have passed sometimes? Why is that? I don't feel they have gone very far at all. I think when you focus on the loss and how much you miss them then you can't find them but if you are more connected, having fun, and enjoying life you can feel them with you.

Intuition Vibing

How do I tune into it? This can be a bit confusing at the beginning. Sometimes you hear other random words or voices in your head. I find that it's more of a subtle feeling. A knowing that this is the way to go. It feels like loving, wellness, and goodness. It's more in the heart space and the gut. The heart holds so much information. It flows from the center of the Universe through your heart.

We tend to focus on what's around us, what's right in front of us, and of course who can blame us? There is overstimulation overload on this planet. The beautiful colors, the objects, the scenery. I mean, it's magnificent. You also have billions of distractions every day including the internet, social media. It's highly logical that you would find it hard these days to tap into your intuition. You can see why they say so many cultures that still live off the land and under the stars have amazing instincts because they are not overloaded with information. Never fear, it's not too late for you to learn how to tap in. You just have to filter the overstimulation out.

It's important to have awareness and check in with yourself every day. I would say to try as much as you can. Take a bathroom break at work and just use that time to reconnect. Close your eyes and take some deep breaths. Check in when you're making a decision. Does this align with what I want? Does it feel good? Try and keep your vibe high when you're trying to tune in. It's very hard to trust that it's your intuition if you're feeling angry and watching frustrating, dramatic programs. You could really be vibing with those kinds of thought forms still floating around or other lower vibe energies.

I mean, don't freak out because the lower energies are just like an annoying neighbor and a frustrating family member. They are there but you don't have to hang around with them all of the time.

Just Be You

I love this message I have heard on an Abraham Hicks podcast. You are having exposure to new experiences. You are asking for things that you desire and the Universe is bringing it to you. Your soul becomes one with your ideas. The contrast in the world helps you really decide what you like. You are completely worthy. You're finding your preferences daily through life. Through the good and what you might call bad.

Your soul is always with you, always guiding you. The contrast provides you with new desires. We have millions of dollars waiting for us. We just get deterred from our dreams and think they can't happen, so it doesn't physically manifest, or it takes a long time.

We ask for what we want. The Source of the Universe knows what you want. You must become a vibrational match to what you are asking for. You have to figure out how to become aligned with something you want. So what you want is waiting for you because you have visualized it and it's in the vibrational environment that you can't see because it hasn't physically manifested yet. There's a thought before anything takes form. But the problem is we are here complaining about what we want and what we don't have. We aren't a vibrational match to what is waiting for us. It's all there waiting, but we are putting resistance on it.

We came in as babies as pure positive energy, but our signal isn't as strong. Our connection to the Universe isn't as it was because of the powerful vibrations, denser energy and contrast on earth. By the time we come from the center of the Universe through the stars and the Milky Way we are on a different frequency. We can find our connection again. Meditation helps clear all of the distractions on earth.

We have come here as an extension of the Universe. The Source. The energy that creates worlds. We are helping to expand the Universe so it can see who it can become. The emotions you feel are about the vibrational relationship you have with your soul. When you're angry, you're not in alignment with your soul. When you're stressed, you're not in alignment. You have to stop watching the news, complaining with the complainers. Stop getting frustrated when you can't control a situation.

All of this makes so much sense as to why there are so many different cultures, colors, races, and gender identity. It's so amazing how many options of who you can become are out there. I think it's such a beautiful mix of what we can be. What the source of the Universe can be. We can love anyone, be who we are. We don't need to prove anything to anyone else. You can't wait for the rest of the world to catch up with who you are.

What's the point of trying? You are on the leading edge. You can be whoever you want to be.

Some people, parents or other associations might not believe that it is ok to be who you are. It doesn't matter what they think. It just matters that you are happy. They have just become stuck in the old paradigms. They are still holding on to the past belief systems. Just be who you are and stop trying to get everyone to understand you. You waste your precious energy. Just role model how amazingly unique you are. I think it's so awesome that people are being their true authentic selves.

We have not been sent here as inadequate humans. We are not here because we are broken, and we need to prove our worthiness. We are not here because there is something wrong with us. We came because we are creators. The Source of the Universe is loving the experience and expansion we are providing. We are like children learning and growing and finding what we like.

Over the years there has been so many people that have been called crazy or weird when they have different experiences or "gifts." Some people were uncomfortable with psychics, mediums, people that "channel." A lot of people are reluctant to talk about it because of past belief systems. I feel it comes from a lot of misunderstanding and misinterpretation. They are receiving information and all of us can do it. People are calling it mystical, but it is actually normal.

Books from the past, movies, religion, tv shows used to make it seem like it was not ok for a normal human to use their own energy, their power, their intuition. In my perspective all that is happening is that we are using more than the 10 percent of our brains that most of us are told we only use. I believe we can utilize our brains in so many more ways. Things that used to be called miracles, or witchcraft are actually neurons firing in our brains and linking with the power of the Universe.

We are connecting to something bigger than us, but it's a part of us. I also feel you can connect to unwanted things, and this is what scares people a lot. I feel that in the middle of the Universe it is pure goodness. I think what you connect to on this earth depends on your intention and how you are feeling. If you want to connect to "scary things" or something that others would call negative, then that's what you're going to get. But if most of the time you are focusing on good, fun, loving energy then that's what you will let in.

I also have to note that depending on your energy or the person reading your energy they might be tapping into different frequencies or reading their own energy so make sure you feel comfortable and a feeling of calm and trust before getting advice. Personally, I like to live in the present moment as much as I can.

I am definitely still in the discovery stage. That's why I love learning about quantum physics because it continues to uncover how "superhuman" we actually are. Nothing bad is going to happen to you if you tap into your brain and bodies capabilities.

Have you noticed that people are getting stronger, faster, more capable than ever before? We are advancing physically at extreme rates so why wouldn't our brains be advancing as well? I kind of don't want to say evolving because I feel the potential was always there. We are just finally unlocking the secret. I mean, some incredible people have been doing this stuff for centuries but we call them exceptional, geniuses, or miracles.

History also damned others as well for using their potential brainpower but I don't want to go back in time. It is what it is. I would love to leave all of that in the past. If you want to focus on all of the wrongs that have happened in the past then that's what you're going to keep bringing into your future. It's a complete misunderstanding. We are living in the present moment so it's more about educating people rather than repeating history again by keeping it alive.

Why is it so crazy and scary that we can advance our brains and bodies and be a stronger, more aware, alert, creative, healing, intuitive human being?

It's time to see how amazing we really are. It's not just stories from myths and legends. We are the legends. We are capable of so much more than we can ever imagine. Society's beliefs on certain subjects have slowed the energy down but I think now it's time to get past the weird, scary factor. Athletes are often tuned into their full potential. It's not just physically, but it's mentally as well. How do those people go underwater and hold their breath for so long? It's mind over matter literally. We aren't just matter; we are also energy. So if you become more energy you can become more you. The more in tune you are with yourself the higher the energy. The more stressed and disconnected you are the denser the energy which means your body is more physical matter which makes you feel bogged down and heavier.

Everyone gets downloads. Some people say, "Get in the zone." When athletes are tuning into their potential, the energy flows through them. When artists are in the zone, the energy flows through them. When mediums are in the zone, the energy flows through them. All of us can connect to so many different frequencies/energies/vibrations. Which ones are you connecting to? It's like a radio station. Which station are you tuned into? The station depends on the frequency.

I know this stuff sounds a bit crazy but years ago so did the internet. Your brain is like a receiver. The way you feel is what you will tune into. If you're feeling angry, you will get the frequencies of angry stations. If you are feeling good, you will get the frequencies of lighter more playful stations. It's hard to explain. You just have to keep allowing it to flow. You need to feel it. Those radio waves are energy/frequency/vibration. We are atoms, particles/waves, so we are energy, frequency and vibration. Like a magnet we can draw in similar energies.

All of your creating starts off with energy. After a while the energy from what you're putting out there—your feelings, your thoughts—start to manifest into something physical. So if you're calm, you have clarity from mindfulness, meditation, clearing the mind, then you have the energy you require to create and it's the energy you want to put out for your creation.

But if you're all stressed out, angry and frustrated then that is the energy you are putting into your creations. Now I'm not saying this is wrong because some amazing creations can come out of anger and frustration but what would you rather do for your body in the long term? A buildup of anger and frustration can lead to injuries and illnesses. These are stuck emotions and blocks.

You need to find your own guidance. It's an amazing feeling when you don't have to rely on anyone to make you feel good. It's fun finding people along your path that might have interesting therapies or you can buy something that makes you feel good but in the end none of that stuff can do as good of a job as what you can do for yourself. You can sit and find yourself and let the energy flow through you. The pure positive energy of the Universe has the healing properties. It has the clarity, the focus, the inspiration, and the creativity. You just have to be ready to receive it.

You have strong intuition and inspiration flowing through you. Do you feel sometimes that you had an idea, or you wrote some sentences, and you have no idea where that thought came from? That's from the Universe. You can tell the difference between a thought that's from the Universe and a thought that has come from some random energy because the Universe is pure positive thought. It's fun, it's inspiring, it's exciting, it's easy. It feels good. It flows. You want more of it.

CHAPTER 3

MANIFESTING YOUR DREAMS

"The most floored of all floored premises is 'The more you do, the more you are worth.'"

- ABRAHAM HICKS

Money + Relationships

Let the universe provide you with what you deserve. Let the money of the Universe allow you the freedom to enjoy life. You're creating a life to be happy but why don't you just be happy now?

A large number of people believe that there's not enough money for everyone. They believe that they have to work hard to prove their worth. Lately, I keep saying work smarter not harder. Life is meant to be enjoyed. There is enough money for everyone. It's all up to your perception and what you put out there.

You can focus on what's going right or you can focus on what's going wrong. It's your choice.

Before you can get what you want you have to get over how you're feeling. You have to get over not feeling satisfied. You have to get over feeling disappointed. You have to get over feeling frustrated. You have to get over feeling like you don't have enough money. You have to stop worrying that you don't have a relationship. Things won't flow to you easily if you have blocks in your way.

Optimism takes you into the now and where your future self really is. Look at things that are easy to feel good about. Don't lose sight of your dreams because you are looking at what's happening around you.

Do you wonder why the same things happen to you over and over again? It might be little things, or it might be big things. That's because you've got something activated in your energy, your vibration. You get what you think about. If you're not feeling good about something or you keep talking about the same thing it keeps it in your experience. That's why history repeats itself. We keep reliving and talking about the same stuff.

There's vibrational history that just keeps coming back. It's the same patterns of thought. Meditation can help clear things. Mindfulness is an excellent tool. Focus on good things and appreciate as much as you can. What is the root cause of why the same things are repeating? It will just keep going and you will be stuck in a cycle until you let go of resistance that you have on subjects. Don't try too hard to figure it out because you can keep activating the same stuff but just try and let it all go. To do this, you just need to relax. Don't try too hard. Just be content where you are. Be content with your body. Be content with your work. Be content with where you are with everything. When you can just relax every day more and more good things start to happen. You find the clarity for the relationship or job you want. You find the strength to do something that you thought you could never do.

If there's something you're interested in, maybe work-wise or something else you're trying to figure out, then make sure when you first start getting ideas that you're in a good frame of mind. What do you think the frequency is that you're putting out there? Is it a lack of money? Because the job you end up with could go the opposite way. It's extremely important to care about how you feel in order to find the right job, bring in money, relationships, and places to live.

Before you can fall in love with someone else, you need to fall in love with yourself. In order to make your dreams happen you have to feel it. You have to look at what you want like it's already happened. Feel what you desire. Become it. Taste it. Feel it. Be it.

We have the freedom to choose what we desire. The Universe doesn't hear our voices, it speaks in vibration. There are so many languages, but it all begins with vibration. Everything you see, touch, smell, hear is vibrational. If you are emitting a frequency of having a lack of money, then that's what you will have. If you worry about money or feel you don't have enough, then that's what you will have. It's the same for any subject.

Some of the top athletes and moneymakers in the world visualize already having something or doing something. Loving it before it has actually happened.

Instead of focusing on how you can't get the ball in the hoop, visualize it going in. The same with money. Visualize already having it. Play games where you mentally spend your money on things that you've dreamt of. Feel it. The more resistance you put on a subject the more you will feel a lack of something.

Keep practicing every day on feeling good, feeling abundant, feeling worthy and connected with your inner self. Trust in your intuition for guidance. Unless your story is purely positive, stop talking about all of the things you've done wrong or your ailments or injuries. Stop talking about your struggles.

Start talking about what you have, what you appreciate. Start talking about how you would like your future to be and visualize having that.

"Real magic is not about gaining power over others: it is about gaining power over yourself." - Rosemary Guiley

Are you satisfied where you are? Sometimes we get what we want. We've been trying to get it for so long and then it finally arrives and that's it.

Now you are onto the next thing. It's boring having what you want because you always want more. This is why some say it's "about the journey, not the destination." You need to enjoy getting there. The fun of looking for a relationship. The pleasure of making money. You just need to enjoy the process because once you have everything you ever want, you will just want a whole load more stuff after that. Just enjoy each step. If you relax and just chill, then things seem to flow in more easily. You're putting a barrier on things if you're focusing on it not being there.

Money comes through alignment of thought. Do you notice people making heaps of money without hardly doing anything? Financial success doesn't require hard work. You need to direct your own thoughts. Don't look at money as a bad thing. Money is freedom. Don't look at it like you have to have it. Think of it as something that helps you explore, grow, and discover. Don't feel uncomfortable when spending money. The feeling of shortage slows the flow of money. There is no shortage of money in the Universe. Don't feel guilty about wanting or having money. You deserve it. You're not taking it from others.

You can't look at things you don't like or don't want and still feel good. However you are flowing, your energy is what you're going to get back.

Look around and when you see things you like, write it down. There's a car you want. A job you desire. Start getting an idea of what you like as a person. Feel yourself in the car and having that amazing job.

Mastering Emotions

"Happiness depends upon ourselves" -Aristotle.

Emotions are very important. We need to discern our emotions properly. You don't know what you're working on if you're not listening to your emotions.

Identifying and expressing your emotion can be a bit confusing some days. We don't know how to feel the emotion. They are thought clusters, photon light particles. plasma (charged matter), subatomic particles (interaction - electricity). Over time you can create misaligned chemistry of the cells.

You are in charge of your emotions. Everything is purposeful. Your emotions are an amazing tool. They are an intelligent system. You can use it and master it.

Be aware of where your emotions are coming from. How are they making you feel mentally and physically?

Your emotions and how you feel matters. The action you take will depend on your own personal belief system. One person that is angry may take a completely different action from another. It's dependent on how you grew up and what you have learned.

Experience what is happening. Allow the emotion to come to the surface. Recognize your emotions. Interpret what your guidance's message is. You can then make a decision on what you want to create. We need to stop blocking our feelings and find ways to positively release them.

(Teaching inspired from - Caroline Cory website omniumuniverse. com)

What you are trying to create might not be your true essence. Make a decision about what you might want to create. Don't think about the job or a project. Think about what you really want. It doesn't have to be specific.

"I want to be happy. I want to have time to play. I want to have the money for freedom." Create a reality that is fun and enjoyable. You hardly have to do anything. We are overthinking everything.

Our brain channels are electrical signals. Put it out into the Universe that you are open to new, exciting experiences. Everything we do sends an electrical signal out into the unified field. Make a decision. You want to create something that's in alignment with who you are. You just need to start with the basics. Your brain channels will align.

You don't need the whole big picture. You don't even need the steps of where to start.

"I want something that is going to be in alignment with who I am." Keep focusing on the basic things you want. Visualize having it.

Happiness, abundance, wellness, excitement. Whatever makes you feel good. Just put it out there into the Universe.

You will start to get more clarity on what you want and what it will look like. The job ideas will start to come. The money will start to come. The relationships, the house. Just get in alignment. A place where you feel satisfied where you are.

Why do we have feelings? If you are not supposed to feel, then what's the point of feelings? You can learn to feel your emotions and release them, then move up to better feeling emotions.

We get used to not allowing feelings to come through. Think about ways you can release blocked emotions. Exercise, meditation, mindfulness, healing practitioners, music, yoga, tai chi, podcasts, laugh, sunlight, art, creative experiences, feng shui, healthy food, unplug from devices, rest, sleep, yoga Nidra, crystals, nature, surfing, breathing techniques, pets and much more.

We are all here to create something different. It's up to you to decide what works for you.

People have learned behaviors. Sometimes people have been brought up with violence, so they feel in order to fix something then violence is the right thing to do. This is what they have been taught. This is why I find it hard to condemn anyone because they believe they are doing the right thing. This is what they have grown up with. This is what they believe. It is a continuous cycle.

They see external things that show it's unfair. So they are teaching each other a lesson. They are trying to fix things but it's in a violent way. The learned behavior has been taught that violence is the way to fix things. You think people are cruel or heartless but it's their learned behavior. They think they are doing the right thing. They aren't processing their emotions properly. In some people's minds, they have the logic that what they are doing is right.

When you give attention to something it ends up part of your vibration. You need to clear your vibrational energetic clutter. It's like spring cleaning your house.

Is this something that is a positive addition to my experience? Is it useful? Is it beneficial? Is it wanted? If the answer is not yes, then put it in a vibrational box. What are your thoughts saying? If you feel they are blocking you and are unwanted, then put those thought blocks in an unwanted pile. An inactive pile.

"I don't have enough money."

"I will never find love."

"Nothing works out for me."

"I don't often feel good."

Or

"I am abundant."

"I am loved."

"Everything is working out for me."

"I am wellness."

What does your pile look like? The Universe will keep bringing you things to add to your pile. It gives you freedom. So, you can choose to have a "negative" pile, or you can choose to have a "positive" pile. Set the things aside that give negative emotion when you think about them.

Just because you think something is true doesn't mean you have to give attention to it. What vibration are you putting out there? Are you stacking up a wall of resistance and not letting what you really want to come in? Every time you talk about what you don't want you put a block in your way. Eventually, these blocks can lead to physical injuries or illness.

Can you deactivate the unwanted pile of blocks and keep activating beliefs and thoughts that feel good?

Try not to focus too much on the unwanted. Just briefly think about it or write it down and send it away or store it in an inactive box. The other day I started visualizing bricks. I was hitting them with a hammer in the air. You may want a softer approach.

Commercials, news and so many things can make you feel bad. Where do you want to resonate? On the "good" or the "bad"?

Every thought creates a vibrational version of what you want, but you can become impatient and put resistance on your dreams.

You need to trust and stop clouding your thoughts with doubt and worry.

Thoughts, feelings, and beliefs have a certain frequency. The dominant frequency gets reflected back to you, so it shows you what's in your energy field.

Have you ever felt like there's a part of you that is the best of you? It's beyond your experiences. The knowing part of you.

Do you wonder if children see more "magical" things because they are on a higher vibration? They laugh, they play. They haven't put all of the resistance on themselves like we do as we get older. We can still play like we are children. Life is so much more fun and freer if you let go of the unwanted thoughts.

You might not feel worthy of having an abundance or having a great job, but you definitely are. You are far more worthy and loved than you know.

Reset

Now is your time to reconnect with the earth, yourself, and the people in your soul tribe. The Universe wants us to care about ourselves and others. It's best to focus on what we do have and not what we don't have. Stop and reset. Think about what's really important instead of rushing, stressing and not fully enjoying life. It's about the connection with the little things.

Mindfulness means maintaining a moment-by-moment awareness of our thoughts, feelings, bodily sensations, and surrounding environment, through a gentle, nurturing lens. When we practice mindfulness, our thoughts tune into what we're sensing in the present moment rather than rehashing the past or imagining the future.

We need to fully be in tune with ourselves and our bodies, then we can start putting our dreams, wants, and loves out there. More money comes in and relationships start to blossom. If you're not in a good space in your head and your heart you will only receive that back into your life. You'll attract the wrong person. You'll attract someone that is in your same vibration. Care about how you are feeling.

Vibration Shift

Manifesting what we want is simple. It takes perseverance to understand how easy it is. All we have to do is ask for what we want; however, there is a catch. The energy we put into asking affects what we manifest. If we ask the Universe for things in a desperate, needy, or doubtful way, we will actually attract more despair, need and doubt. You have less money coming in if you are doubting you will get it. You will have less money if you're begging for it. Same with a relationship. In addition, if we are too vague about what we desire we can end up manifesting the wrong things or nothing at all. We can also ask for too much at once, not allow it to come in, then get overwhelmed.

With money, visualize yourself spending it. Money gives you the freedom to do what you want to do. You are deserving of it and there's definitely plenty in the Universe to go around. It's such a human thing to worry about money. It's our currency so it would be normal for us to overthink it.

With a relationship, focus on what that person would feel like to you. That person is kind, fun, loving, generous. Visualize what you want, not what you don't want. Really think about what you're putting out there. Some people are putting out the wrong kind of vibe. You are saying you want one thing but you're really wanting something completely different.

This is why it is important to get very clear about both our energy and our intentions before we attempt to manifest our desires. It's the perfect time to tap into our souls. Don't just let it pass you by.

You are always on your path; you just have resistance. You don't have to get bogged down with others.

Can you shift your vibration to stay in alignment with your true self and be the person you are truly meant to be? You may be stuck in cycles of unwanted vibrations. It's not your fault. It happens to all of us, but you can get out of them. Every day you can catch those negative thoughts. You can focus on what makes you happy. Think about what REALLY makes you happy. Stop saying I can't do that. Or that will never happen. Stop getting caught up in other people's drama or the world's controversy. Your reality is what you focus on. You are not ignoring problems or not caring. Wanting to feel good should be your highest priority. The Universe would prefer you put out vibrations that are positive, uplifting, joyful, peaceful, loving. Why would you want to send out the vibrations of negativity, unworthiness, worry, stress, anger, frustration, doubt, sadness? Imagine if the whole world started putting out more positivity. It would be an awesome party. Let's start with ourselves. There's no better time than now. Love yourself and the Universe will feel the shift. Just care about feeling good.

The contrast is so huge in this world that it's helping us understand desires and dreams that we didn't even know we have. So it's expanding our consciousness in a far greater way than ever before. This life isn't a clearing process. It's a place to create and have fun and enjoy the physicality.

Our consciousness, some call it soul, higher self, inner being, source is always with us. Part of our consciousness is here on planet earth and part of it is in the non-physical realm. There's not as much disconnect as we all think. When we become satisfied with our lives and release as much of the resistance we have, then we can tap in more to the non-physical part of ourselves. It's connected to so much more. It guides, it's intuitive, it's knowledgeable, it's amazing, it's you. Can't you see that the days you are happy things are flowing and you feel more creative. Everything seems to work out for you? It's that simple. Happiness allows you to see your true self. Your magnificent, incredible self, that you're not realizing that you are.

Tune in to the subtlety of receiving.

It's said that we are all conscientiousness connected as one like a lake. You can scoop a cup of water out. We have soul family's that stick together. Focusing and helping others that have the same interests. The masters, the artists, the musicians of the past can all flow through us when we are aligned and fully connected to our true selves.

The energy we are made from is pure divine love. We hold it in every cell of our bodies. Some of us have forgotten. Can you feel a flow of energy running through you that is pure? Tap into your heart and feel that love. You can become more calm, resilient and happier. We don't need to get love from anywhere or anyone. Although that's nice as well. We've had it inside of us all along. It's in our DNA. We bring it to every situation. Treasure your own magnificence. You are more loved and worthy than you can ever imagine. We are divine love.

If you were bullied or teased at school, it often comes from the way you are feeling about yourself. Get over the insecurities and start owning your amazing flaws. Imperfection is so beautiful.

I'm less willing to take myself into negative conflict because I know it doesn't serve me. With friends or family, depressing or sad movies. It's just not worth lowering your vibration.

Remember not to feel bad if you judge someone or judge yourself. We feel bad sometimes because we've judged someone that's judging others. You have to understand that everyone has been brought up with different beliefs. They may be saying some not so nice things about others but who were their role models? It can't feel good to them to be saying mean or controversial things. It's best not to get yourself out of alignment by getting angry or frustrated at them. It's just a vicious cycle of everyone being angry and frustrated. Before you judge yourself or others just remember you haven't lived in their shoes. We don't need to all be the same. We can all have our own opinions.

People want to feel good. They have a path that they veer off sometimes. We can't have everyone on the same wavelength. Look for the good points in others. Nobody is perfect.

Your brain has an electrical signal. Everything you do is going to send a signal out into the unified field. You don't have to know exactly what you want. What relationship, what job. You just need to release all fears. You just need to make a decision to create. You could say: "I want to make a decision about creating something that is aligned with who I really am." You don't know what it's going to be, but you need to be open to receiving the right information. You simply decide to create something you want. You'll start to get more clarity on what it is and how to get it.

It's all about your mindset. There are those that suffer at the best of times and those that thrive at the worst of times.

Life is about happiness and enjoyment. It's not about suffering. It's up to you to take control of your inner world. You've got this!!

CHAPTER 4

"GOOD" VS. "BAD"

*"The mind is everything.
What you think you become"*

— BUDDHA.

Polarity + Duality

Life may never be perfect because of duality and polarity. We need "good + bad" days. (I don't like to call them bad days because there is always some form of growth and learning.)

We need a bit of the negative to push us on the right track. If we lose our way or we are on the wrong path, we may feel that nothing is going our way. But actually, it is. The Universe is slightly nudging or hugely pushing you to get back on track.

The more you become conscious through mindfulness, meditation, appreciation or whatever works for you, the more you will recognize that there aren't any coincidences. You are the one that has manifested something happening. It can sound completely crazy, and it does take a while to understand it, but you get back what you put out there. Your thoughts, feelings, and emotions create your own reality. Cause and effect.

Our visual spectrum is very small. If you are at a lower frequency, you attract lower energies. If your vibration is higher, you cannot attract that different frequency. Sometimes when we are tired or have so much going on, we can easily have lower energies weighing us down.

It's ok. It's not a bad thing. The energies just waste time and distract you. If you try to keep aligned with the higher frequencies, then you don't have all of those tagalongs. You can detach the lower-level energies.

They can make you feel down and give you anxiety. They are thought forms, energies, and lower beings.

You can clear your own space. You can ensure you are at a higher vibration. So you're out of the muddy vibration with all of the draining energies and you're higher up the field with all of the flowers.

A lot of lower emotions can bring you down. That's why it's good not to lower yourself to other people's levels. If you're with the flowers, and you go down into the mud with someone who's angry, sad, or frustrated then you're just going to get stuck in the mud and depending on how you are feeling, the momentum might keep you down in the mud for a while.

Empathy is looking at something and someone and holding yourself in that discomfort. It feels so much better to send people love and have compassion rather than bringing yourself down with them. You can help them so much more with love and compassion. If they are dragging you down, then you just have to focus on yourself, and the right answers will come.

With empathy, you go down to meet them but with compassion, you stay who you are. It's great to practice feeling what emotion you might be on. Are you on the frustrated, overwhelmed, or worried emotions or are you on the contentment, hopefulness, optimism or higher, right up there with love, freedom, empowerment, joy?

"Everything has beauty, but not everyone sees it." - Confucius

History Repeats Itself

It's very hard when we are stuck in old paradigms where we are looking at wars and we keep reliving them. We go around thanking people for their service which in fact these poor soldiers are all killing each other or hurting each other and suffering. Should we be thanking them for killing each other? I know it's very hard when we are stuck in a vicious cycle of people feeling they need to defend their countries, their rights, their lives, their religion. I'm sure we as a collective can come up with better solutions. I don't want to disrespect what so many people have gone through. The PTSD people get just shows you that this is not good for anyone. They lose their lives for us.

If we keep encouraging people to go to war and keep celebrating past wars, then that's what we will keep getting. I think focusing on solutions is so much more powerful than focusing on problems. My little brain couldn't comprehend where to start. Luckily, I don't have to solve the world's "problems." All I can do is just focus on the positive going on in the world.

We can make a difference if we put out the energy of peace. If more of us do that, then we are sending it out into the Universe. The soldiers are only trying to help. If we as a collective can put out more positive vibes then that is far more powerful than one negative person. I see soldiers trying to educate and guide and support. I just love that.

It's not all bad because out of war comes great solutions. For me, though, I would prefer the solutions to come a bit more peacefully. People always think they have to fight against something to get their point across and to have their own way. You can create something much bigger with the connection and power of the Universe. You cannot have a peaceful protest. It's contradictory.

Be Careful What You Wish For

There's the saying, "be careful what you wish for," and it's definitely true. If you're stressed and don't want to work and you say, "I NEED A BREAK" and you break your toe, this is the Universe giving you what you want because you have the freedom to ask for that. Don't panic, you're not going to break your leg just saying it once. There's a huge build-up of thoughts, feelings, and vibrations that has gotten you to that level. Your stress, overwhelmingness, and exhaustion is building up over time. You will get warning signs first, more subtle experiences telling you to slow down, until after a while you have not listened to your intuition, your body—your guidance system. Some say if you stabilize too much—a stable job, stable relationship—then you can't evolve so the Universe pushes you forward to help you evolve and keep moving forward. If it's something stronger like a crisis, then it pushes you towards evolution. We don't really want to experience a crisis, though. We can still evolve through the contrast that is already here. We live in balance by having positive and negative.

You can be the victim, or you can be the creator. Your soul is on a creative journey.

When everything is going bad, it's not because there's a bad force in the Universe. It's because you were so far away from yourself that the energy is pulling you back. It's pulling you back to find your center again. You can see yourself from different perspectives. You can create your own reality. Everything is evolving all of the time. The only constant is that everything is inconstant. Everything is moving and transforming itself.

"In nature, nothing is perfect, and everything is perfect. Trees can be contorted, bent in weird ways, and they're still beautiful." - Alice Walker

Vibe High

The higher the vibration the higher the frequency to put you on the path to manifest your dreams.

If you are always angry, stressed, guilty, or grumpy then your vibe is lower, so the things you want in life take more time. It takes more effort to achieve things. Along the way you can be so stressed that you create diseases and injuries because your body is using your precious healing power on stress rather than building the immune system to become stronger and heal.

We also need to feel emotions. It's important to have the human experience but once we have felt the emotion, then we can let it go.

Negative things are responsible for our growth and development so don't be too hard on yourself if you make mistakes or get angry at the Universe for something that has happened. The negative contrast of bad things happening can often launch us into the space we want to be in. Just think about where your energy is going. Take time out and ask if it is really worth wasting your energy any longer on things that don't help or things that have happened in the past. We need to move on in order to create the life we want.

We can put our energy into education instead of being angry and frustrated at others. Give people the possibility to heal themselves from their "negative" past.

Instead of saying this is bad say, "What do you think about this? How would you solve this? What can we do better?" Put your energy into the future rather than trying to change the past.

We can learn from past experiences as they are amazing wisdom. If you are frustrated, angry, worried, sad, or anxious it could mean you are out of alignment. People feel they have separateness with other individuals. Some people think they are alone, and no one understands. It is far from that. People aren't distant or different from you. We are all here to continue to create this amazing Universe. Some people just have different ways of going about it. It would be incredible if we could all get back to the peaceful place we started from.

It's said the Universe does need duality, positive + negative to help us evolve, but sometimes we stray too far. I don't like to call things good or bad. Some people just need education and love. I don't believe there is a "bad" place we go to when we transition because I don't believe anyone is "bad." They need help and education. A lot of people in prison have had negative role models that have taught them over time. I feel a lot of people have just lost their way.

If we are angry and frustrated at someone that is angry and frustrated then what is that putting out into the Universe? What vibration is it creating if everyone is fighting and protesting about peace? I'm not sure how we've gotten to the place where we feel we have to fight, yell, and scream to prove a point. We can achieve so much more when we work together.

To get back on track, listen to what makes you feel good. It doesn't have to be buying expensive things, or going on trips. The outside world is awesome and fun, but you don't need money or fancy events to reconnect with your soul. Just love the "simple" things.

It's very hard to judge who's right or wrong because people are believing what they are saying and theirs is the truth. You may think they are completely wrong but in their mind, they feel they are completely right. It's their perception and their belief. Does that make them a liar or wrong? Eyewitness accounts come up with completely different stories because how people have perceived the situation can be a completely individual take on the subject.

There is no reality that we can agree upon. Everyone's reality is different because we see things differently. We smell things differently. We taste things differently.

We have been taught that this is how things taste or sound, but everyone tastes and hears and sees slightly differently. If you ask a writer to get information off the internet and say, "Make sure you get the truth," what is true? Because someone says it's true, does that really make it true? Is it true because you believe it? But what if someone else doesn't believe that?

Sorry, I'm probably confusing you and I don't want to overwhelm you. I just think it's best not to get really stressed or worried or overthink everything in life.

A doctor can tell you that you're more than likely to get a disease because a family member did, but is that true? Or are we tricking our minds to believe that it's going to happen? We just need to be more aware of what we are actually telling ourselves. You can literally trigger your genes from what you are telling yourself, so focus on love and kindness towards your mind and body. Don't walk around saying, "I'm probably going to get sick."

I just saw a mother online whose child is ill, and she kept saying, "His heart is broken." Why would you tell a child something like that? So in his mind, he thinks he's broken. Wouldn't you rather say, "You have a beautiful heart and every day we are working on making it stronger." I don't feel we need to tell a child they cannot heal or that they are damaged.

Put your hand on your heart and reconnect your brain and heart coherence.

After watching Matias De Stefano on Gaia.com, he claims he remembers where he came from. He said the Universe created positive and negative so we can be pushed forward. It helps us evolve otherwise we would just stand still and not ever move.

Positive X Negative

You need a good life balance. There is polarity. Positive and negative. Light and Dark. If you're being pulled toward one too much, then you will get lost in one of those perspectives, and the Universe will hit you from behind. You have two forces to create realities, positive and negative.

If you are working too hard, using more action, then the Universe will keep sending you signs. The energies will try to remind you that you are out of your way, varying off your path onto a bumpy road. This is where accidents can happen because your body over time just needs a break. It tries to tell you to slow down and look after yourself but finally if you don't listen something can happen. An injury or an illness occurs. Please don't worry, panic, or overthink it. You can say those things and have bad thoughts. It's just a huge build up over time of being stressed out, angry, frustrated, and worried that can eventually lead to a literal break or mental breakdown.

Also sometimes a broken bone or mental breakdown can actually not be as bad as a heart attack, so the Universe slowly shows you that you need to slow it down. You can still have an extremely busy life, but you can enjoy what you're doing. Even if it looks like a bad job to some people, you can still enjoy it. You can be cleaning toilets and having the best time. You could be a celebrity and be absolutely miserable.

We are passionate, powerful creators.

It's the journey that is the fun part. We can't be holding ourselves to unrealistic standards. We won't always be spewing sunshine and light. We can acknowledge there are things that we want and things that we don't want.

It's great to make the best of every situation. It's not great to amplify something unwanted and deliberately increase the direction of something unwanted. We can experience contrast and choice. A vibrational attitude of knowing. When you want it and believe it you are getting close, but you need to want it and know it!

You have turned the negative emotions around and you just focus yourself into a vibrational attitude that feels good. Too much deviance from who you are doesn't feel good. Too much negativity gives too much variance from who you are.

You have the capacity to live in this physical body feeling good and being really well, as long as there are things that keep steering you to new expansion and you're keeping up with it fairly well. The things that go wrong occur when the Universe is stirring up expansion and you're not going along with it. Make sure you have enough variety. Over time you will figure out what's calling you. If you don't find things that make you feel good and you keep stressing and don't release the emotional energetic blocks in your system then you can end up feeling unwell.

We see doctors and scientists literally scaring people to death by telling people they are ill or only have a certain amount of time to live. I've been told many times, "There's not any disease that is incurable." The doctors are trying to help. You just can't take anything as set in stone. Do what you need to do to get help from a doctor or health practitioner while you continue to work on yourself. Seek other opinions and advice.

I used to find when I had pain somewhere I would take some anti-inflammatory pills. I would try to block the pain and hide the pain, hoping it would just disappear—ultimately not allowing the innate wisdom of my body to heal itself. Inflammation is the body trying to repair and heal itself. I would push the pain deeper and cause it to last longer than needed.

No one should have to suffer or go through unwanted things, but it does make us stronger. I found if I calmed my mind and focused on my body I could visualize myself feeling good. I would take a deep breath and breathe into the pain instead of holding it tight. It's more of a release of that energy. A block of emotions can store up as denser energy resulting in pain. If you can start to release that block then you can get some relief. I would focus on my wellness rather than my illness.

The challenge is that sometimes the emotional blocks aren't where the pain is. It's more of a referred pain type of thing. We don't want to stir too much up and keep reliving old situations. You can just go around in circles trying to go deeper into your past to figure out exactly when the block started. You just need to intend on releasing it and try not to just fixate on where the pain is because your knee might be sore, but the culprit is your blocked emotions in your kidney. You might be feeling frustrated about something so your elbow is aching. Any conditions you have whether it's skin conditions or something else can come from your emotions.

We find so many reasons not to move in the positive direction. You get disheartened and don't continue in the direction you want. Pay attention to your own guidance. Get a handle on your vibration while you feel good.

The Universe Is Looking Out for You

Sometimes you may think something has gone wrong but actually, it's gone really right. It could be the Universe helping you and saving you from something worse. You are running late because you can't find your keys, but it might mean you end up missing an accident. You need to listen to yourself. If you're not looking after yourself and you're getting really stressed then you can end up in worse situations.

Extreme contrast is when you're asking for something but you're not allowing it. You're ignoring what you're asking for, or you are not open to receiving it. You don't think it can really happen.

If life were predictable, it would cease to be life.

Process emotions by reaching for a better feeling thought. If you're now is not pleasant, then daydream. Your inner being and the Universe is divinely cooperating with who you are. Negative emotion is telling you that you've asked for a lot but you're not letting it in. You are not in the receiving mode. You are not letting things flow to you. For example when you ask for more money but you're complaining about how much you don't have.

Life comes when you make mistakes. It's like you are constantly a child learning and growing. You don't 'Need to be taught a lesson!'. Your learning as your growing so what you go through is your lesson.

We are on 'Earth School'. We are leading-edge creators of the Universe.

Your main purpose, I believe is to find what you like and what you don't like. To connect with your soul and cooperatively work together with the energy of the Universe. Through contrast and mistakes, you make, you find what you enjoy which shows you who you really are.

At this moment in time, you are where you wanted to be. We all benefit from the contrast that's happening around us. Life doesn't move forward as much if we are not motivated by things we want and what we don't want.

It's such a beautifully diverse planet which makes it exciting to non-physical. It's an amazing place to grow your soul. They say we have deliberately chosen this life. It can challenge and inspire and teach us what we can truly do, who we can be, and what we really enjoy and love.

All of the exciting stuff is happening before you actually get something. Can you imagine if you just visualized something and poof it appears? Can you imagine if you wanted to do an art class and the teacher completed your art, and you didn't get to try it or practice or enjoy it? You have to appreciate doing things on the way to achieving something. That's the fun part.

Dilute what you don't want with what you do want. Focus on what you want rather than what you don't want.

After focusing so much on what makes me feel good I really notice when people use words that lower their frequency. By trying not to focus on your problems you're only amplifying the problems. By focusing on what is going well then you are highlighting the areas that can bring in more abundance.

The Universe brings you what you want. You need to get ready for it. It will be bringing you things daily but if you're in a grump, you could walk straight past what you're asking for. You don't need to know exactly what it is you want but you need to be open and get ready for the Universe to bring it to you. If you are stressed, closed off, angry, depressed then you're not going to see the signs or let it in. It's like you've closed the door and everything you want is hiding behind it. You can't see anything but it's there.

You were born into the contrast for the purpose of making choices. There is always going to be contrast. Always going to be things you don't like or things that are stressful, but you have the choice to react or not to.

Contrast is expanding the Universe so much more than if life was perfect.

CHANGE YOUR LIFE
BY CHANGING
YOUR THOUGHTS

Paramahansa Yogananda

CHAPTER 5

WELLNESS ABSORPTION

*"Relaxation means releasing all concern and tension
and letting the natural order of life flow
through one's being."*

- DONALD CURTIS

All of us come into this world fresh, excited, connected. We're ready to create, expand, evolve, and have fun then adults come along and tell us how they think it is. "Life is hard. Wait until you get older. Money doesn't grow on trees. It's not all about you."

It's great to spend time resetting the mind. Getting past all of those things we were taught as kids. I believe you can have money. Life doesn't have to be hard and being older is awesome because you can buy what you want from the shops! I'm very lucky. My parents are awesome and have always let me do what I want. They are positive people, so I have definitely had an advantage. It's not too late for you. We can't change our parents, but we can stop blaming them and trying to live up to their expectations. You can be your own person.

It's Not Just physical

Focus on the different areas that need a bit of rest. If you can balance your physical body, mind, and soul then you are more likely to get what you want and deserve.

I've seen a number of people talk about the different types of rest.

Physical Rest

You know when you are physically exhausted. You struggle just to keep your eyes from closing. Catching up on physical rest can mean focusing on your breathing. You may not be getting enough oxygen into your blood and lungs. Maybe you need to be doing some more calming classes at home or at the gym instead of constant cardio. You may have overdone it. You need a massage to release tension or aches. Maybe some meditation classes, Yoga or Tai chi, stretching, Yoga Nidra. A spa sounds good.

Mental Rest

Do you sometimes feel like your brain is in total overload and you don't even know what day it is? You try to think of a name and your mind goes totally blank. Complete mush. Maybe you need some mental rest. Turn off your screens and find some way of grounding yourself again. Go to the beach, go for a walk. If you're at work, just close your eyes for thirty seconds and take some deep breaths. Think of things you appreciate. Think of the basic things in life that you love. You might have some little quick meditation to go to. Have you got a saying or a mantra? I am strong, powerful, amazing. Make something up that makes you feel good. I prefer to say something positive rather than saying, "I'm not tired," because you're bringing that feeling of tiredness in so you keep it active.

Social Rest

Sometimes other people can be completely exhausting. It's not their fault. You might be tired and have a lot going on. Going out and socializing or being in chat groups or Zoom all day can be a lot. Don't feel bad completely ignoring your friends for a little bit. If they're your true friends, they will understand. Sometimes it's not just your friends; it's social media. It's pretty crazy how many hours we spend surfing the web but then we say we don't have time to relax, meditate or do yoga or do what makes us feel good.

Sensory Rest

You can also be looking at the computer, phones, iPads, and other screens so much that your brain is overstimulated. You're wired. You may need some fresh air. Don't forget to utilize the natural world for a feeling of relief. If you can't get out just close your eyes and breathe.

Creative Rest

I feel these days we are always on a creative mission. You may say you're not creative, but you are constantly creating. That's your mission here on earth, to have fun creating. You're thinking of new ideas and new ways to do things. You can always make time in your day for a quick break.

Spiritual Rest

You'll know what's right for you in this area. Go for whatever feels good. If you're unsure and it doesn't feel good, then try and calm your mind and find what resonates. There are so many amazing communities out there that will have ideas and passions similar to yours. Just give yourself a break and find your own connection as well. Do what works for you. We are all unique, so you don't have to follow in someone else's footsteps. You might be seeking a sense of purpose. You can do this by having some loving time to yourself. Self-care. Quieten the mind then the Universe will bring you something supportive and fun.

Emotional Rest

Saving the best until last. We don't realize how important emotions are. They are an indicator that something is wrong. They are our guidance system. They are telling us the areas we need to work on. If your emotions are on a lower level, then you need to be looking at the above areas so you can rest and hopefully start to lift your emotional vibe. Let go of trying to do things for everyone else and start doing things for yourself.

Meditation

Meditation means; To become familiar with. I say appreciation and joy are the key to unlocking happiness but probably in my mind they are equal with mindfulness and meditation. Mindfulness and meditation are the most amazing tools you can use to help you with success in all areas of life. It can also help illness and physical ailments, reduce blood pressure, anxiety, stress and so much more.

I used to think that meditation was just for monks and people that were a bit random. It is far from weird. Scientifically, it opens neuro pathways and connections. If you want more advice and explanations about the benefits in a scientific respect there are many physicists and experts that have been experimenting and researching this area. Dr Joe Dispenza is someone off the top of my head that has spent hours and hours doing MRI, ECGS and way more authentic research.

Doctors and scientists are proving the benefits of meditation daily. You are building quantum coherence. 95 percent of who we are is a subconscious program. You can become conscious and stop living in a program. Don't give up. Keep trying. When you start noticing your thoughts you are observing them so that's an amazing victory.

When you do this, instead of responding and getting up and quitting, then that's a victory because you're in charge of your mind and body. It's creating synaptic connections within your brain. In meditation, you get less sensory information coming into the brain. You can check your emails and get food later. You have opportunities to connect and visualize the future you want. The future that is already there waiting for you.

Can you find the present moment and focus on creating a life that you enjoy? Can you get past the analytical mind? We need to find a place where our environment isn't controlling our thoughts or our body. Where you place your attention is where you place your energy. So if you can spend time with yourself and reconnect you can put more energy into your body and help build your immune system, your brain coherence, visualize the future you want to see and so much more.

So much of our brain is taken up with habits, behaviors, programs, attitudes, and beliefs. It makes up who we are. The analytical mind is navigating through life. We need it for our jobs, driving, and making decisions. But we are becoming over-analytical. We can get behind the mind and the unconscious beliefs and start to reprogram our brains to have a more enjoyable life experience.

Meditation can be a powerful tool to get you on your way. When you first start it can be like an electric sensation with the power of pure positive energy surging. It's a lightning bolt of magical energy. We don't realize how out of alignment we can be physically, mentally, and energetically.

In meditation you can feel like you're floating because you're moving into a higher vibration and becoming less physical matter. So you're lighter rather than denser. This can definitely freak some people out at first, giving them an anxious feeling. The heart expands which feels like something is wrong. Relax into it. Feel it and continue. It's the most amazing expansive feeling. If you keep practicing, you will eventually get there. Don't try too hard. The more you relax and stop trying the easier it is.

Your thoughts will go crazy at the beginning, and you might try to stop your thoughts but just watch them and stay seated. You may try for a little bit longer than the first day. I started seeing my thoughts as pixels on a big tv screen. I felt like there was a door behind my thoughts. Finally, after a while I got behind the thoughts then there was a peaceful stillness. A calmness. A blissful feeling. It's amazing. It's like a drug. A natural high. You just want more.

There will be days where you can't be bothered feeling good so you may not meditate, or you may only sit for a minute but over time if you keep persevering you realize the difference it makes in your life. A lightness. A peacefulness. The world can be on fire around you and you are totally calm and happy. There's a knowing that even through the chaos of the world that everything is going to be ok. In the end, nothing is really wrong.

Some days I get full of inspiration. My dreams and desires come to life, so I struggle to sit for long but that's ok. I can't hold back and I'm on a mission with all of these fun ideas, words and experiences to focus on.

At the beginning you really need to keep practicing. Just settle your body down. The inspiration will start flowing.

You need to find what resonates with you. Through my research and my own practice, I see it can strengthen areas of your brain responsible for memory, learning, attention, and self-awareness. It's said that meditation can also help calm down and support your sympathetic and parasympathetic nervous systems. (The sympathetic nervous system is involved in preparing the body for stress-related activities; the parasympathetic nervous system is associated with returning the body to routine, day-to-day operations.) The two systems have complementary functions, operating in tandem to maintain the body's homeostasis.

Research is showing that mindfulness & meditation can increase cognitive abilities, memory, and attention. Meditation is "giving your brain a break for a minute."

In the silence, it will be revealed who you really are.

It creates calmness, contentment, happiness and clarity. Excitement and inspiration.

We all have excuses not to meditate. I don't have time. I have kids. I have work. I just have this thing I need to do. The thing is, when you do start to consistently meditate then you find you clear the unwanted random thoughts. It's like you've checked heaps of things off a to-do list. Your mind has so much more space. You have clarity and you achieve things with more ease and flow. I used to say I didn't have time to meditate but if you checked my phone, I was on social media, and Google for hours.

Now I don't need to be aimlessly drifting through the net when it feels like it is all coming to me naturally.

When you finally get past your mind, it's so clear. It's like you're looking at yourself and the world from a higher position. Up on a huge mountain. The view is clearer. There's not a bunch of random stuff floating around in your brain. It's like cleaning out all of the old unwanted software that is totally outdated in a computer. Stuff from years ago that's not relevant anymore and is making it sluggish. It's moving slower with so many apps open and unused obsolete data. Meditation just helps to clear all of the old and then you can receive fresh ideas and inspiration.

While writing this book I started meditating for longer periods of time. I was doing more healing and cleansing type meditations to release old thought patterns and emotional blocks that I could have had stored from years ago. You can easily hold on to old emotions. Feelings of guilt. Sadness from something that has happened. Anger, frustration. There's so much that we have all been through in our lives you would expect to have a bit of stuff built up.

We don't need to carry the fears and traumas of the past into the present. We can reprogram our brains. You could be scared of dogs because a dog barked at you when you were a two-year-old. You might not feel worthy because a teacher told you that you did a bad job. So many little things build up and add up to be big things. Someone tells you that you don't look good then you end up being paranoid about your weight or your skin. It's so crazy how much other people or things can influence the way our lives are.

Don't let any of that old baggage mess with your mind and body anymore. Find a way to release it. Let it float away with the clouds. Bury it into the soil and turn that into energy for the plants. Do whatever feels right for you. When you can get rid of the old, then you are ready for the fresh, more inspired, happier you.

After doing a bit of cleansing daily, I then started to get inspiration for this book. As soon as I got on a roll with downloads of ideas, I couldn't stop and I was finding it hard to meditate. I was so excited that my brain just had constant words and ideas flowing. I'm in the receiving mode. I'm getting the inspiration to do something I've wanted to do. A dream, a desire is coming to life because I took the time out for myself.

I started off doing some meditations, including Dr Joe Dispenza, Abraham Hicks, meditation podcasts on Apple and Spotify. Gaia TV has different options. I also love doing meditations with Yoga teachers. There are also plenty of options out there now for meditation groups to support you on your journey. It's really great to quieten the mind and have nothingness, but it takes practice to get beyond your mind and thoughts. In the beginning, I found it helpful to start with a bit of guidance. Some people just watch a flame or listen to a sound like a bird or feel the breeze. It's beneficial to have more of a consistent sound as well.

Some days I was excited and did it for one hour and other days just fifteen minutes. I think a good amount of time is fifteen to twenty minutes, but if you've only got five mins, it's better than nothing.

You can also do mindfulness walking and other meditations during the day. The fifteen to twenty minutes with eyes closed really do make a difference because it gives you time to clear your thoughts and have time to connect to your soul. It's your practice, so it's totally up to you how long you want to do it. Just having that quiet time in your mind allows so much clarity.

I can't say enough good things about meditation. In the beginning, some people feel a bit scared because they don't understand it. There's been so many stories, movies and beliefs that could have made you unsure or uncomfortable. People calling it mystical which makes it sound unnatural. Just keep going. Nothing bad is going to happen to you.

Some people may cough at the beginning. I've often heard it said that a cough can be a release of old blocks. Sometimes you can feel tingling, heart expansion, coolness or heat. Feeling movement in meditation is the neuroendocrine system moving throughout your body. There can be many different sensations. Once you break through with your meditations, it's the most blissful awesome sensation. It's a feeling you can't even describe. Just persevere.

Sometimes I wonder if some people's anxiety is them connecting to energies and they are not understanding and relaxing with it. Also, anxiety can be your guidance system telling you that you have to care about feeling good. It can be when you're stuck in a lower vibration and you're feeling everyone else's anxiety as well. In order to get past anxiety and reach higher, better feelings, I would recommend meditating.

"Opening to Universal frequencies."

I have been told that the tingling and ringing in ears and other sensations is when you're connecting to Universal frequencies. It's a very high frequency. You are downloading a ton of information. Because it's so far away and we have forgotten how to interpret its vibration it's not heard on the normal hearing spectrum. It's not coherent.

If you allow it to integrate within your cellular makeup and relax, you will translate it into information that is clear to your physical brain.

It can tell you:

♥ Who you are

♥ What you're doing

♥ Your connection to creation

You hear of people not eating before they meditate or people fasting. My interpretation of this is because food can weigh you down. When you meditate it's like you float up higher (not usually literally). Some people can levitate but I certainly haven't reached that level yet. So when you meditate you reach higher frequencies/vibrations. Different foods have different vibrations, they have a different frequency, so if you're putting more unhealthy heavy foods in your body it can weigh you down. That's just how I interpret it.

I'm not saying don't eat because I love food. I had a huge meal the other night before meditation and it was great. I try not to overthink it. I definitely won't be fasting anytime soon. Check with a healthcare professional if you're ever thinking about fasting.

The value of meditating, just having that quiet time in your mind allows so much clarity. The high, the buzz you can get when you finally learn to meditate with ease is the most blissful feeling. I can get that feeling all throughout the day, but it did take practice. Don't give up because it's not working straight away. There are layers of learning, discovering, and evolving you're being. Like an onion, you peel away each layer. It's the same with anything. The more you practice, the more it comes naturally or easily.

You might actually be meditating already, and you don't even know it. If you're a long-time meditator, then that's great. Hopefully, more people tune in. There's a huge number of people that meditate and they don't even realize it. This one podcast I listened to involved this guy talking about a famous rapper, asking why the rap star was so rich and he doesn't meditate. Abraham Hicks described that rapping and music was this famous person's way of meditating. The energy flows through him while on stage or in the studio. You might find you meditate in other ways apart from just seated meditation.

For me, I love starting fresh and meditating in the morning before all of the resistance of the day has built up. I go out of the house fresh and clear. I still really enjoy meditating at other times of the day as well. I think just do what works for you.

If you're looking at different options, I really love Yoga Nidra. You can listen to podcasts or music. It's super relaxing. If you don't know what Yoga Nidra is, then you should try it sometime. It's pretty much just like having an afternoon catnap. You can also do it just before you go to sleep while you're in bed. It doesn't matter if you fall asleep. You just lay down in a comfortable position. You can be on a yoga mat. I actually love the grass in summer or the couch in winter. I like a blanket because I cool down fast. Do it however you like. It's your practice. Why would you be uncomfortable because someone says you have to do it a certain way? You get to choose.

Yoga Nidra is a form of guided meditation, a method of Pratyahara (withdrawal of senses) that allows you to scan the body and tap into a state of relaxed consciousness as the mind settles in a place between wakefulness and sleep. It is among the deepest possible states of relaxation while still maintaining full consciousness.

According to *Yoga Journal*, 'Richard Miller is the pioneer responsible for bringing the practice to a remarkable variety of settings' which includes 'military bases and in veterans' clinics, homeless shelters, Montessori schools, Head Start programs, hospitals, hospices, chemical dependency centers, and jails. The iRest protocol was used with soldiers returning from Iraq and Afghanistan suffering from post-traumatic stress disorder (PTSD). Based on this work, the Surgeon General of the United States Army endorsed Yoga Nidra as a complementary alternative medicine (CAM) for chronic pain in 2010." (Wikipedia.org)

There are also heaps of meditation podcasts. They are amazing at bedtime. I just set my timer to turn it off after fifty minutes but I'm usually asleep in the first ten minutes. I definitely fall asleep if I do Yoga Nidra in bed but that's ok. If I fall asleep, I must have needed it.

Just try it sometime. Don't worry what anyone else thinks. Don't let conditions confine you. Be free. Be who you are. Don't go looking for the rest of society to agree with you. Be who you want to be. Pushing against something only makes things harder. You don't need to please everyone else or wait for everyone else to please you.

You can expand your consciousness in the energy field. Align the mind channel with a higher frequency. You can align it with the frequency of source. The frequency of the Universe. You simply intend to connect to the frequency. You can receive healing and clearing. Ask your mind to just quieten down. Allow your thoughts to just stop. Keep practicing. When you think about it we are actually energy beings. Everything in the

Universe is energy. You are part of the consciousness that is creating this world. You are helping to make this world bigger.

Remember to look after yourselves. A lot of us are sensitive souls. Empathetic people who are passionate and care deeply about others. We take on other people's pain, fear, emotions, and it can be really draining on our physical bodies. You can feel sick, get headaches, anxiety, feel completely stressed out, dizzy, panic attacks, and the list goes on. If you are feeling any of these things just take time to breathe. Get into nature, meditate, relax. Do whatever you can to calm yourself. Try to send negative thoughts out of your head. If we panic or stress we can send more negative energies out there. Send positive thoughts and love from the top of your head to your toes. Send it to your friends and family and the rest of the world. You need to stop being empathic and start being compassionate. You are not helping anyone by lowering your own vibration.

Have you focused on how you feel? Reach for good feeling thoughts. If you feel good, then you will bring more good into your life. If you are focusing on negativity, then you will bring more of that into your life. Do you watch the news all of the time? Do you get frustrated if your partner doesn't know what clean is? Do you watch dramatic tv shows? Whatever you are focusing on you will just bring more of that into your life.

The law of attraction reminds me of Google and Pinterest. It brings you what it thinks you want. If you're angry, it will bring you more people that are angry. If you're vulnerable, it will bring you more things to make you feel even more vulnerable. You have to care about how you feel. If you want more money, then you are saying you don't have money. You need to visualize already having things. All of us put blocks on our true desires by focusing on negative things or not believing we can have what we want. Start every day trying to feel good. It's actually easier than you think to feel good. You just have to let go of the resistance and be mindful of what you're watching, listening to, talking about and how you're feeling. If it doesn't make you feel good, don't watch it or talk about it. Just have fun. I highly recommend meditation to help guide you to a better life.

Foods & Supplements

I'm still on the discovery stage with food and supplements. I'm not trained and I'm still trying to interpret everything for myself. Personally, I feel that once you have connected with your own inner guidance system then more things just fall into place.

What works for one doesn't work for another so who am I to tell you what's going to work for you? I would love to just have a clean slate and get rid of all belief systems about food. There are so many advertisements, books, and media, telling you that this is "good," and this is "bad." We are so confused about what to actually put in our bodies. This again is all perception. If you think it's bad, then that's what you are telling your body. If you think you're overweight and keep telling yourself that and you're telling all of your friends you are overweight then you're telling your mind and body as well.

I learned a lot when I was really stressed out and overwhelmed about seven years ago. I was just trying to get through the day. Not breathing correctly. One hundred things on my to do list. I started to feel so tired. I ended up going to a few evenings with Nutritionist Ben Warren from BePure New Zealand and he explained about adrenal fatigue and how we get into a fight, flight, or freeze pattern and it can affect our bodies. He had some great tips on mindfulness, and he explained how it's common now that people aren't getting as many nutrients and minerals as they need in foods. We have beautiful fresh fruits and vegetables but in a lot of places the natural vitamins and minerals have been depleted. It's good to ensure you are getting the right balance. I didn't want to rely on having to take any supplements but sometimes a top up of good vitamins can get you started or keep you going when you are just really struggling to feel good. I find they continue to help balance me out. At the beginning

I really needed a vitamin B top up and Zinc. I love vitamin C for the immune system and healthy-looking skin. It's totally up to you and I would check with a professional.

I believe if we are totally connected and at one with the energy of the Universe we probably don't need much at all but that's not reality. For me, I know a few vitamins can support me to give me that extra boost. We are exposed to a lot going on daily so don't feel bad about getting a bit of extra help. Check what's right for your needs. I also met an amazing woman called The Holistic Pharmacist. She really helped put me on the right track. She took an overall approach to health and wellbeing, mindfulness, and the importance of breathing and relieving stress.

She discussed the "vagal tone." (Vagal tone is an internal biological process that represents the activity of the vagus nerve. Increasing your vagal tone activates the parasympathetic nervous system, and having higher vagal tone means that your body can relax faster after stress.) You don't realize how amazingly beautiful and complex your body is until you start to unravel how it works. We really take it for granted.

Sunday is the perfect day to take time out or think about what you can do in the future to help yourself. So many people these days have anxiety and mental illness. It's not a bad thing, it's just not nice to have to go through it. There are so many factors which cause it. We don't need to live in fight or flight and freeze all day just because we are stuck in traffic. The main thing is to just put yourself as number one. If your tank is full, then you can be ok for everyone else in your life.

Take time for yourself. Go for a walk. Go to yoga, gym, fitness class (whatever you enjoy). Don't put more stress on your body by overdoing it! You see some people working so hard running at 5am and spending hours at the gym, but they put on weight because their body is stressed. Find a balance. You can use sage, palo santo or sweetgrass to get rid of negative energies. Mindfulness is an amazing tool for all of us. Breathe. Reset. Live in the now and be grateful for everything you have. Meditation can also clear out your brain, just like having a spring cleanout. Sweep away all of the old thoughts that you don't need. The past is the past. The future hasn't happened. Now is the only time.

Someone that really helped myself and my family was Georgia from Georgia Ella Homeopathy. I still feel even with the power to utilize the pure positive energy of the Universe it's not always realistic to do everything on your own. I love how homeopathy utilizes the natural world to create healing and calm.

Georgia talks gut health:

"As Homeopaths, we don't just rely on treating physical health or healing the gut. So many nourish their gut yet still have ongoing issues. We go deeper to explore overall health. Why are the symptoms flaring and what are they trying to tell us?

"What is causing the immune system reaction or lack of? Is it the environment, stressors, trauma, medications, the birth process?

"Appropriate supplementation, nutrition and healthy gut flora are super important, but why are so many people doing all the "work" yet still falling victim to a compromised immune system?

"With homeopathy we can address all layers to help clear blockages and weaknesses. We unravel and peel the layers, addressing what comes up stage by stage. It's a freeing experience, one where you get to know yourself on a much deeper level.

"Homeopathy is similar to TCM (Traditional Chinese Medicine) in the fact that it works with energy and helps move anything stagnant causing blockages and the symptoms we express.

"If you can start to view the emotional and mental body as one with the physical, it will help to unlock so much for you."

Georgia Ella Homeopathy https://georgiaellahealth.com/

Stop Being So Hard on Yourself

Would you tell anyone they look bad, they are overweight, too skinny, terrible skin, fat thighs? I mean, the list goes on. Stop being so mean to yourself. Stop judging yourself.

People judge from their own place of insecurity. What you think about you bring about. There are two ways to show power. You can push people down. Or raise them up.

Children are coming in with a stronger sense of who they are. Don't focus on the way others are behaving. Just notice the way you're feeling. You can control how you feel and what you tell yourself. You need to start being kinder to yourself. People will reflect back to you how you are feeling.

There's a vibrational reality. It's gathering resources until it manifests. Visualize how you want your life to be. Look for the positive aspects about everything then you can come up with a better solution. By focusing on the unwanted you just continue to draw in more of that. The same works for everything.

Renee Rigden from Renee's Kitchen New Zealand talks about self-care:

"It's not just about what you're putting into your body. Make a promise to yourself, or buddy up with someone to hold you accountable to what you say or do.

"Schedule into your calendar your commitment to look after yourself and set a reminder of things you can try at home.

"'Self massage,'" Om Rub, tiger balm, oils or body moisturizers you have in the back of the cupboard, dry skin brushing.

"Pop a few drops into Epsom salts before your bath for increased relaxation. Add a carrier oil or "fragrance free" moisturizer 1/10 and rub onto the soles of your feet in the evening or anytime of the day. I am no essential oil guru but I do enjoy them. I use a sleep and calm oil blend regularly. (Epsom salt baths use 1-2 cups. A great way to absorb magnesium, great for the whole family.)

"Be kind to yourself, commit to no negative self-talk for one day. This is actually hard—but we should practice this more. Say one kind thing to yourself each time you walk past a mirror.

"Let go of perfection, but do something each day that you know lifts your mood, makes you feel good.

"Get creative in the kitchen, put ingredients you have into Pinterest for recipe ideas. Pull out/dust off cookbooks, make wholesome, healthy vegetable packed food.

"Come up with a plan if you feel overwhelmed.

"Take yourself somewhere where you can have some quiet for a time. Aim for connection not perfection with kids if you have them."

www.reneeskitchen.co.nz

Water

The more water you drink the more easily energy flows.

Benefits of drinking water:
- Can be carrying nutrients and oxygen to your cells
- Flushing out bacteria
- Aiding digestion
- Normalizing blood pressure
- Stabilizing heartbeat
- Protecting organs and tissues
- Regulating body temperature
- Maintaining electrolytes
- And much more

(Health.Harvard.edu)

Focus on telling yourself that you are healthy, fit, young, and feeling good. Tell yourself you're amazing until you start to believe it.

What you tell yourself is making a difference. You're drawing from your life force. You can work on releasing stuck emotions. For example for pain in the hip you could try telling yourself positive things:

Hip release

"I am able to process, metabolize, and release all emotions."

"I am in perfect balance."

"I release any fear I have stored in my hips!"

"I move forward in life with ease and with joy at every age."

"I release any anger I have stored in my hips!"

"I am free to move!"

"My hips are strong and healthy!"

"I allow myself to believe I deserve to heal."

You can do this for any area that you have concerns about. It can be hard at the beginning to shift negative thinking to positive talk. Just try one day at a time and reflect back at the end of each day. What could I have said next time? What would I change? What positive words could I have added? Please don't overthink everything. Just intend on releasing it and let it go. It may be coming from other area's so focus on whole body wellness not illness.

"How to Activate Your Happiness Chemicals"

Melissa Jade from Facetime Skin Clinic New Zealand talks about Happiness Chemicals:

"We should be treating our brain the same way we treat our bodies. That means taking specific steps to care for it as best we can.

"Naturally occurring chemicals in the brain shape our emotions and the way we process the world around us. Today we are talking about how to activate these 'happiness chemicals' to exercise your mental health."

Serotonin
"The Mood Stabilizer."

Serotonin impacts every part of your body, from your emotions to your motor skills. Serotonin is considered a natural mood stabilizer and is thought to regulate anxiety, happiness, and mood.

How to activate
- Practicing meditation
- Spending time in nature

- Getting sun exposure
- Exercising and being active

Dopamine
"The Reward Chemical"

Dopamine is a neurotransmitter made in the brain. Basically, it acts as a chemical messenger between neurons. Dopamine is released when your brain is expecting a reward or when you associate a certain activity with pleasure.

How to activate
- Celebrating the small wins
- Eating a good meal
- Taking time for self-care
- Completing a task

Endorphin
"The Pain Killer"

Endorphins are involved in our natural reward circuits and are related to important activities like eating, drinking, physical fitness, and sexual intercourse. Endorphins also surge during pregnancy. They minimize discomfort and pain and maximize pleasure. This helps us to continue functioning despite injury or stress.

How to activate
- Laughing out loud
- Volunteering and giving back
- Exercising and being active
- Watching a good movie

Oxytocin
"The Love Hormone"

Oxytocin is a hormone that acts as a neurotransmitter. It plays an important role in reproduction. One review of research suggests that oxytocin has a positive impact on social behaviors related to relaxation, trust and overall psychological stability. Oxytocin has also been shown to decrease stress and anxiety levels when released into certain parts of the brain.

How to activate
- Physical affection
- Giving a compliment

https://www.facetimeclinic.co.nz/

Try and become a creator of your life and not a victim of your life. Your personality creates your personal reality.

Thoughts and feelings influence every single atom in your life. Don't focus on anxiety; focus on feeling good. Don't focus on your illness; focus on your wellness.

CHAPTER 6

SOUL PURPOSE

"You are here to enable the divine purpose of the Universe to unfold. That is how important you are!"

- ECKHART TOLLE

Your soul is on a creative journey. You are always on your path; you just have resistance. You don't have to get bogged down with others.

Every thought has created a vibration of what we want, but we need to be patient and let it manifest in the physical world. It takes time to sync up with your dreams. There's so much doubt that we have. We worry, we stress, we get frustrated, so this slows it down.

We are all energy. We are consciousness creating this amazing world. Everything in your life is what's going on in your energy field. Everything is being reflected back to you. You are more than your physical body. Can't you feel that there is something else within?

You have your own personal view of the world from all of the experiences you have lived and created. Can you feel that there's something deep within you? The best of you? It's there with you always. Your soul, your inner being, higher consciousness. Whatever you want to call it. You can tap into the field of all possibilities. A field of unbounded consciousness. It is beneficial to connect with yourself. I totally recommend meditation. It takes you beyond where the answers lie.

Breathe in, breathe out. Let everything go. Let all tension flow out. Breathe in filling your body with oxygen. Breathe in life. Breathe out and let go of everything unwanted.

What means more to you? Being true to who you really are or pleasing others? Being the person you're meant to be or pleasing your parents? You can satisfy other people but in order to find your alignment you have to be yourself and do what works for you. Otherwise you lose your own clarity if you're trying to be accepted by everyone else. You're not here on this earth to please everyone else—you're here to create, explore and expand yourself.

You may feel that what you do is insignificant, but it's far from it. The simple things you are doing in life is expanding the Universe at a greater rate than ever before.

Suffering and sacrifice is not a good way to live. That's not what I would call really living, just trying to get through your day.

Can you shift your vibration to stay in alignment with your true self and be the person you are truly meant to be? You may be stuck in a cycle of unwanted vibrations. It's not your fault. It happens to all of us, but you can get out of them. It can take time because you have so much momentum going in the opposite direction. Every day you can catch those negative thoughts. You can change the subject because sometimes it's extremely hard to stop thinking about the things you keep thinking about. You can focus on subjects that make you feel good. Think about what really makes you happy. Stop saying, "I can't do that" or "that will never happen." Stop getting caught up in other people's drama or the world's controversy. Your reality is what you focus on.

You are not ignoring problems or not caring. Wanting to feel good should be your highest priority. It is ok to allow yourself to feel good. The

Universe would prefer you put out vibrations that are positive, uplifting, joyful, peaceful, and loving. Why would you want to send out the vibrations of negativity, unworthiness, worry, stress, anger, frustration, doubt, and sadness? Imagine if the whole world started putting out more positivity. It would be an awesome party. Let's start with ourselves. There's no better time than now. Love yourself, and the Universe will feel the shift.

Just care about feeling good. You have to decide to find the vibrational frequency of ease. Find the path of least resistance. The path of most allowing. You are on your path, but how much resistance are you putting on your trail? Find _ease_ instead of ending up with a dis_ease_.

What you resist persists.

The Universe flows through your heart. Do you get goosebumps, excitement, a feeling of bliss? Does this happen daily? The more you do things for yourself, the more you can have magical moments daily. You are truly incredible. Goosebumps are telling you that you're on the right track. You are allowing the energy of the Universe to flow through you. It means you are in alignment.

Are you wasting time trying to find your soul purpose but are not sure where to start? Are you already on the path to finding your full potential? Or are you just wandering around aimlessly trying to navigate the world around you?

Are you being guided, are you in the receiving mode? You can tell when you're getting the right guidance by the way you feel. If you're feeling good, tuned in to your body, then you receive the right thoughts to get you on your path. You can feel when you're being guided. It just feels right. Ask yourself, have I been guided and is it going to help me or someone else? Don't worry if you veer off your path. Like a GPS in the car your guidance will pull you back on track again. You just have to practice being satisfied, appreciating and caring about how you feel.

As a being, as a soul, you are seeing what you can become. Believe in yourself. The only goal is to know yourself. The whole Universe is in the perfect balance. You can realize that you can transform and create your own reality. You can start to understand every perspective that you have created. Living in this world is like living your dreams. This is the most important dream you could have created. You've come to experience what you have created. Unfortunately we get caught up in everyone else's realities and we lose our way a little bit. We get unwell or we are stressed but all of this contrast is setting us up for knowing what we really want. Not getting it now doesn't mean you're never going to have it. Some say that everything that you ever want and dreamed of is waiting for you on the other side. The contrast that earth gives us really helps us determine our exact preferences. It's like putting your favorite songs in a playlist. It's all there waiting for you.

"You must be the change you wish to see in the world." - Gandhi

You can have compassion for the things going on around you, but the only way you can really help others is to get into alignment. You can't help others if you're not helping yourself.

You may not be on the exact path, but all of these roads lead you to your destination. If you can get out of your own mind, then you can have the most incredible journey in the place we all call home. The place that brings us all together as one. The beautiful round sphere we call Earth.

We have the power to experience a moment in time where we are the designer of our destiny. We can create a moment on Earth where we are on an incredible path where the world is not our enemy; it is our protector.

Sometimes challenges can expose our special gifts. You have talents and creation abilities. It's important that you recognize and share your gifts. Are you aware of your special attributes? They can lead you on a path of success. Let others inspire you but let your path be your own. Take the best of what you've seen and merge it with your individual desires.

We have the privilege of living this human experience. Why not make the most of it! Planet Earth is where it's at. The leading edge planet where we can bring our dreams to life.

Manifesting what we want is simple. All we have to do is ask for what we want; however, there is a catch. The energy we put into asking affects what we manifest. If we ask the Universe for things in a desperate, needy, or doubtful way, we will actually attract more despair, need and doubt. In addition, if we are too vague about what we desire we can end up manifesting the wrong things or nothing at all. For example with a job, you need to intend for the job to flow easily. Be fun. Bring you more abundance. You don't need to know what the job actually is or where it is. Just intend on finding the right job for you. This is why it is important to get very clear about both our energy and our intentions before we attempt to manifest our desires. It's actually best to relax and think less about it. Just expect it to come at the right time. Sometimes when you make too much effort about a subject, it put's resistance on it. This can mean it slows the process down.

Do you hear people talk about "awakenings". It's said they help you to see beyond the illusions and conventional fabric of society, and instead help you to transition into your "true" life that you were meant to live from birth; a life full of abundance, prosperity and happiness. There can be different levels of awakening. Like different levels of a game there are layers of who we are and who we can become.

No person can fully define a spiritual awakening for another. Of course, each person has a different outlook on life and defines things differently. It can happen at any moment or period in your life.

I hear people say that they wished they had awakened sooner but there is no right or wrong time. It's your own journey. Sometimes I feel it's better if you awaken later so you get to have a real physical human experience. It's a completely different world if you are not awakened. Far more contrast which in turn can really help expansion. You can evolve really fast by having the human experience. Don't ever feel bad or that it's too late.

You may not have awakened yet and you are thinking what is this person on about.

When you awaken or are on the journey to awakening there are many different things that happen.

- You seek more meaning and purpose in life.

- You would love to understand who you truly are.

- You realize you're the creator of your life and take more responsibility for your decisions and actions.

- Patterns & synchronicities emerge. You could start seeing numbers or strange coincidences keep happening.

It all starts from within. If you can reconnect to your own body again, then you can reconnect to the world. You may be thinking, well actually I am connected to the world. I don't mean the internet, the TV, or phones. I mean really connecting. Soul connecting. Becoming one with the Universe. This may sound slightly crazy, but all of a sudden, it clicks, and you wake up to a world that is truly inspiring—a world that is working with you to create experiences for you to enjoy.

You could be the roadblock to your own destiny. It's not your fault. It's years of conditioning and belief systems. Things we've been through and what we've seen with our eyes. But is this all really reality? What is reality? Is it your perception of what's happening? You can be next to someone having the exact same experience, but you might be laughing and they might be crying.

How we see the world totally depends on our thoughts, feelings and beliefs. The body is like a character. An avatar. It's an amazing vessel. Without touch, smell, taste, seeing and hearing our 3D world isn't anything. You're downloading everything through your senses. We move our bodies through space and that takes time. Our world is a space and time 3D reality. We have time so that we have places to be, and we have space which means we move from one point to another. Point A to point B. You are the creator of your life. You have to stop reacting to everything that is around you. Don't let the environment control the way you feel. We start relying on the environment to give us a stable feeling and then we end up on autopilot and we do the same old things. We can get behind the autopilot and manifest our dreams.

Create a future that you want. It all starts with satisfaction. If you can't be positive or you can't find things that make you feel good, if you're struggling to find your way, just start with being satisfied. Be content with where you are. You can get to where you want to be faster if you just appreciate where you are. Just be satisfied. You're not going to get to your dreams if you're complaining about where you are.

You're creating a new you. A more powerful awareness of you. A beautiful person that has more knowledge, understanding and peace. You are more in touch with your soul and the energy that surrounds you. The elements are aligning for us to evolve into more beautiful powerful beings. We can reach further than we ever thought we could. Stand strong, you have the strength. You are amazing.

You can get so excited or even overwhelmed sometimes that you have to constantly check in with yourself to see how you're doing. Do you ignore your body and mind and just keep going? Just take a breath and ask yourself how am I feeling today? If you're feeling good, then that's awesome. If you're not feeling good then ask yourself what you can do to feel better. Do you need exercise? Do you need a dish of healthier food? Do you need more water? Do you need some time out? Do you need Netflix and chill? What is it your body is craving?

My Soul Contract?

"We are made from the same fabric as the Universe so within us we have a Universal DNA. As we expand our consciousness, we can connect with the Universe and dissolve anything that's stuck in our bodies." - Caroline Cory

I'm not sure how I feel about people saying we have a Soul contract where we come here to go through something big in our lives. I think we can go through big things, but I don't think we come here to suffer. I think we are powerful creators and we come to this world to learn, expand, and evolve. I think maybe we have specific things that we want to learn but we are evolving beings so we will continue to learn. We will never get it all done.

The opportunities for the Universe are boundaryless. I feel we have areas of expertise, and you can slowly figure those out by ticking off what makes you feel good and letting go of what doesn't feel good. I do hear often that we choose to come to certain places, choose our parents and choose maybe harder situations to begin with so that would be like a soul contract. Before you enter Earth, you look at what you want to do that may help you evolve. It helps you learn what you like and expands your consciousness. It's your story.

General basics are planned by the vibration you have. You have intentions to stay in alignment. It's very general. You are a creator, and you are guided. The details are left for you to discover for your surprise and delight. You can observe this world and choose what you like. What you want to create. What you want to discover. You intended to come to this time and space.

You will never get everything done that you want. So you might as well just enjoy the ride. You can often create by default but there are a lot of benefits though if you aren't quite on your path.

People are thinking that one day they will die, and they have to get it all done. You are eternal beings so you will never get it all done. What's the point of coming to Earth then? It's for expansion and growth. Learning more and discovering. Finding the best of everything. Finding our collection of favorites. Every experience is a clarifying focus.

You can't focus on what you want though when you're focusing on everyone else. Remember who you are.

You didn't intend to stay in these physical bodies forever. People that pass early haven't done something wrong or veered off their path. This life experience could have given them what they came for and then the path of most allowing would be to transition back to non-physical.

(These are teachings inspired from Abraham Hicks podcasts.)

You intended to explore contrast and define what you prefer. You intended to be in a satisfied mode and witness the power of your focus. You can't find your purpose and awaken by pushing against everything in the world.

So many people through organizations or religions believe they have to suffer and be of service to everyone. So many people feel they have to live up to their parents' expectations and rely on feeling good when parents are proud of them. Often they feel they owe their parents.

We can grow through love and joy, not by suffering. Not by serving everyone else. You serve others if you are happy and looking after yourself. You are putting out so much more good when you have positive energy rather than suffering energy. You do not have to try too hard or suffer. The bonus is though if anyone does suffer they are truly finding out what makes them happy, and their soul can recognize exactly what you want.

The Universe is flowing pure positive energy through you. It's sending messages; it's trying to help. Sometimes we have so many desires that we get overwhelmed. If you're asking for help and not letting it in, then that's when the accidents happen. Nobody wants that. You need to let the help in. You might need a week off or a weekend of rest. You may need to do some things for yourself. If you're not listening to your body that is telling you to slow down, then you can end up ill or hurt.

I think you would continuously be updating your soul contract if you have one. You are part of your soul, and your soul is a part of you so wouldn't you "both" want the best for yourselves. It doesn't feel right to me that you would choose to suffer and continually suffer. I think you have the power to overcome anything.

I still feel that the life experiences of suffering can be an amazing leap into areas that you find incredibly pleasing and rewarding. I just wouldn't be saying that in order to live a human life you have to suffer.

In the end I don't think it really matters because we release all suffering and go back to pure positive energy. The other side is said to have minimal contrast compared to Earth. This world we live in has the craziest contrast which actually makes it appealing. It's like going on a roller coaster ride. You know it's going to have ups and downs but at the end you're buzzing and super excited you did it.

I think when we do suffer we haven't found our alignment with ourselves and our soul. Sometimes we get so lost or overwhelmed or scared that we lose our direction. I think it happens to most people sometimes, but I feel you can pull yourself up again easier than you realize.

Personally, I feel there was a lot of suffering in history and religion, so people think that it is the true human way to suffer. If the true essence of the Universe is pure positive energy, then I don't see the correlation to suffering. I see suffering as freedom and people have the right to suffer if they want to. The Universe lets us have the freedom.

I don't want to sound insensitive because obviously some people are caught up in terrible situations, but you see so many of those people from rough neighborhoods, no home, famine, illness, disease. All of a sudden, they find their way up to the top. How do they do it? They have the willingness, the desire and a knowing that there are better things out there for them. If they continue to focus on all the suffering, feeling sorry for themselves and saying they have no food and money then they get stuck in the cycle of poverty, etc.

The rest of the world contributes to this when in fact there is enough money, water, and food for everyone on the planet. If we focused more on solutions rather than the lack of, we could all work together to provide something for everyone in the world. There are people with so many ranges of abilities. Some have come from nothing so how do these people pull themselves up and become billionaires? You say they are just special one-in-a-million types but what makes them different to anyone else? Some people just call it luck. Maybe it is luck, but I still wonder why some people are luckier than others.

You hear of people hitting rock bottom where they have lost it all. That's when they start to climb back up. The reason they do this is they have no resistance anymore. They have nothing to hold on to.

You don't want to have to hit rock bottom in order to start fresh. Whatever stage you are at in your life you can still move up to better, brighter things. Just release all of the negativity. Let go of the resistance you have on anything. Any negative comments. Saying you don't have money. You don't have relationships. I know it's hard not to look at what is right in front of you and ignore it.

You just have to turn the negative around into a form of satisfaction or appreciation for where you are right now. You'll find things won't happen fast enough at the beginning and you will be frustrated because things you want aren't coming but that frustration and worry only slows you down. All of a sudden things start to happen and unfold in an exciting way.

We are all evolving & using our mind, body, and soul to connect as one. Don't be afraid. You are learning to connect with your own energy. You have more control and power than you think. You can move and heal your own cells in your body. Turn inwards deep into your soul to see that magic that you have inside.

If you sit down on a seat next to the ocean, a river, some trees, or a desert what can you see? I mean what can you really see? Are you just thinking about what time you need to get home? What are you having for dinner? What do you have to do next week?

Can't you just "be"? We are human beings. But I keep hearing people saying we are being "human *doings.*"

When we rush around all day, we don't get to be ourselves. We don't have as much time for creative thoughts. We don't have time to heal our bodies.

So many people get stressed over karma from past lives but personally, I feel if we are eternal beings we are just going to keep growing and expanding and learning so we would release it. If you are happy and guilt-free. If you forgive yourself and others for anything you think you have done or they have done, then all karmic residue should subside. If you notice patterns are repeating in your life, then maybe that's your lesson you haven't learned yet. It's not a bad thing. It's like a child still learning to talk or walk. Life might be trying to tell you something so it keeps throwing it at you until you understand that lesson. You can look at most people that come into your life as your teachers. Even your kids if you have them or other people's children. They can test you. Drive you crazy. They are loud, frustrating and feel like they are put here to annoy you but they could easily be teaching you patience, resilience, compassion, love and kindness.

If something happens, or you choose a certain path then maybe that's something you wanted to learn in this lifetime. Bad things aren't happening as punishment. The law of Attraction is responding to how you feel and what you're putting out into the world. Don't you feel in your soul that you're a good person? No one is bad. You're continually like an infant. Stumbling, making mistakes and learning. You're not often going to judge a child. Why would you judge yourself? It's fun to make mistakes because we grow and learn. We can keep repeating old patterns. Life could be trying to tell you something.

You're not learning lessons in a bad way. You're learning what is unwanted. You're learning what you don't like so you can continue to evolve and enjoy what you do like.

Karma is not something that is bad. Karma is all those things you haven't learned yet. It's helping us expand our consciousness. When you have learned things it's called "Darma." Earth is where you practice coherence. It means to find alignment between who we really are.

You experience every possibility of yourself. You are creating this reality to understand who you are. Earth is where we have come to understand who we are through experience. It's an honor to be on earth.

Search deep into your heart, your soul, your higher self. Do you really believe you were such an awful being in past lives that you're going to be punished? Does your heart really believe that you are a terrible person? You are far from it. Everything you have lived has helped you learn who you are. It's helped you understand what you really desire. What you love, what you don't love. Who you can be. You are creating your own destiny. You are designing your world. This is where you can make your dreams come to life. Where the energetic world meets the physical world. Where energy turns to matter. It is such an amazing opportunity to be able to experience a physical reality. Don't let it pass you by. Find your own truth and your own perspective of reality. You can't care what everyone else thinks. You can't be the light and hold anyone in darkness. To be your true divine self you need to love every part of you. Stop reinforcing the things you don't want.

We have been conditioned to think that something outside of ourselves can heal us and make us feel better. Stop surviving and start thriving. Self- prioritize. Let go of desperation. It just pushes what you want away. Really think about what you want. Is it going to make you happy or is it going to overwhelm you? A belief is nothing more than a pattern of thought. Think about what is really going to make you happy.

Complaining gets you nowhere. Anger, fear, worry, frustration will not lead you to who you are. Love, joy, appreciation leads you to who you truly are. Find better feeling thoughts. The better you feel the more in alignment with your soul you are.

Follow your heart. Don't get caught up in the "parental fantasy." What your parents or family members want you to do. Don't be pressured by society. Don't try to appease everyone. Follow your passion. You can't find happiness if you're doing what everyone else wants you to do. We have wonderful gifts. What is calling you? Find your alignment. What makes you happy?

Focus on your potential. So much more comes out of it rather than focusing on a problem. Ask a question that empowers you rather than looking at the problems around you. Change your perception of yourself. Look at life from the mountaintop.

There isn't anything wrong with you. Nothing you have done in the past is holding you back. Get out of the belief systems of the world. You are far greater than you think you are.

Don't get caught up in pseudo success. Trying to be someone you're not to get likes or thumbs up. That's not who you really are. You don't need that to make you feel good. Don't get forced into a box of how you think society wants you to be.

Set an intention to "wake up." Expand your awareness of who and what you are. Why am I here? Who am I? You can start to get an insight through meditation. Quietening your mind so you can hear and feel your true self. Don't talk about what you don't want to experience. Don't live your life worried about what other people are thinking. Don't worry about what everyone else thinks.

Live your passion. That's your gift. That's who you are. Walk in the direction of your dreams.

A life purpose should not require so much effort. It should come from the joy within our beings.

The purpose is to know yourself and see who you can become. So through your jobs, relationships, travels, etc you are seeing who you are. What you like and what you don't like. That is your purpose. You are achieving your purpose daily through everything you have lived.

Our soul doesn't get filled up because of what other people think of us.

The Universal Library: Are There Akashic Records?

"How could you ever be separate from your source if the essence of this source is who you truly are?"— *Gabrielle Orr*

Have you heard of Akashic records? These are said to be pictorial records, or "memories," of all events, actions, thoughts, and feelings that have occurred since the beginning of time. They are said to be imprinted on Akasha, the astral light, which is described by spiritualists as a fluid ether existing beyond the range of human senses. The Akashic records are reputedly accessible to all. (Information from Britanica.com)

It has been said that the Akashic records are a compendium of all Universal events, thoughts, words, emotions and intent ever to have occurred in the past, present, or future in terms of all entities and life forms, not just human. So it's a record of every single thing that has happened in every single Universe, multiverse, dimension. Whatever is out there. A "Universal Library." Can you imagine the readings? What would you like to look at? It would be like going onto Netflix, but you could watch any part of history in any part of time and before time. It's like a vibrational library. Crazy!

"Cosmic knowledge." It's all that was and all that will ever be. It's past, present, and future and future possibilities. The Akashic records are quantum waves. Fields of energy that are invisible to the eye. Anyone has the ability to tap into this intelligent field. You can visualize being in the Akashic records. Get into a peaceful space. Take deep breaths in and out. You can visualize a library or whatever you come up with. You can visualize a book and ask it what guidance you need, or ask "what is my soul purpose." Take yourself on a journey. It can feel like it's in your heart. It can give you a deeper understanding of who you are.

They say we can tap into the Akashic records. We can let that energy flow through us. Sometimes I wonder if these mega intellectuals in the world tap into this humongous library or server. I mean I don't know much about it and when I first heard it I thought the person that told me was a bit nutty. But I really do feel that some days I can tap into a giant web of knowledge. I write and I read things back and I think how did I write that? I had no idea about a subject but what I wrote seemed compelling. Well, I believed it.

The only thing is, do you wonder why everyone interprets things differently? Why aren't we all downloading the same things and then all being on the same page if it's come from one source. What happens is we all interpret these records differently. Depending on what level of vibration you are on the records alter themselves to become relevant for you to interpret. So the information gets changed depending on your reality and your vibration and how you are feeling at the time. It's best to try and let the information come to you rather than trying to find it. We need to be aligned and centered to download the best information for us. We need to be wide open to receive it.

There's a popular phenomenon at the moment called "automatic writing" where you put your hand on a pen and you just start writing. It's like your soul is tuned to the frequency of the Akashic records or any other information on the information highway in the Universe. I mean, loved ones and guides could be helping us write, because they will be part of the collective consciousness for all things.

Who knows? But you should try it. A great time is after meditation or a calm activity. Just sit with a pen and paper. Don't force anything, just let whatever comes to mind flow. It may not make sense for a bit. It may be a poem or a piece of interesting information. It might help inspire you to the career you want or the relationship you've been looking for. You might not be a writer. You might prefer to see colors or may get songs that have messages.

I remember going to a kinesiologist once. She was my doctor's nurse. She told me not to worry then afterwards I got into the car and a song about not worrying came on. I remember a wave of happiness came over me because it totally felt like the song was there for me right at the perfect time, telling me not to worry. You can't describe those synchronicities when you just feel something resonates and feels like it's coming just for you.

Just take it easy at first when you are tapping in. You need to make sure you're in the right space, feeling better about yourself and doing things that make you feel good. Take a moment in the morning to ground and connect with yourself.

They say you can tap into your soul. Your past lives. You can ask to tap into other people's records (you should ask for permission first).

It's an energetic frequency, a vibration that you're tuning into. I do get high- pitched tones in the ears sometimes now because I'm trying to interpret Universal frequencies but they are not like normal sounds so my ears or senses can't quite unlock it yet.

I don't really like to go back to past lives. I got told once I was an Egyptian goddess, so I thought I'd stick to that because it sounds cool, but I think going back can just bring up old hurt and pain and it just reactivates it all again. The Universe is moving forward. The Source of the Universe wants to see what it can be. I don't think it's looking back. It's like an excited child asking, "What's next!"

What else can we become, what can we create? What can we make? Who can we turn into? What can we look like?

I don't want to bring up the past. This is why history repeats itself because we leave those things activated and it just happens over and over again. It's like we are drawn to the drama of continuing to focus on things that weren't helpful. I'm still not sure about karma. Yes I totally believe in cause and effect and there probably are a few stuck belief systems and blocks left behind, but I really don't overthink it. Personally, I feel your soul gets a fresh start. It's your analytical brain that keeps thinking you have to pay a price for past experiences. That comes from human perception. The Source is pure love and positive energy. We are just like newborn infants. You don't hate them and condemn them if they spill on you.

I hope you're still with me and not thinking this chick has completely lost the plot. I'm not saying all of this is true. I'm just saying this is what I've learned on my journey, and it can be really fun.

Yes, a server or library in the sky does sound slightly crazy. But all of our thoughts and experiences are out there. They are energy and energy doesn't die.

You don't think a computer server is crazy or search engines that bring you the information you need. Have we been made to think that we are mere limited humans? We could never have that kind of potential? Science is showing us that we are far more than we think. Our brains are receivers. We can pretty much download what we want.

I found for a while I'd start to believe things and then I'd be in the "real world" with traffic and things to do. All that other stuff seemed so far-fetched like something from a movie. But every day another thing would happen that I couldn't keep saying was just a coincidence. The information and the signs that come when you are more open and aware is so exciting. I'm not sure how many "coincidences" you can have but for me

"Synchronicity happens when we align with the flow of the Universe rather than insisting the Universe flow our way." - Akemi G

A few years ago, I went to a medium. I remember feeling a bit nervous and unsure because of old beliefs. She seemed to know so much about everyone in the group.

I spoke to the medium afterwards, and she looked at me and said, "You can do this you know." I freaked out. I was like no way!! I feel bad because I probably seemed kind of rude, but I was just scared. The stories you hear and the awful movies that humans create leave you thinking that it's from a dark place. Religion often says it's only devils or gods that do things like that. No mere mortal can connect with the Universe. It's a bit old fashioned. Something that is such a human perspective. Old misunderstandings and beliefs over time.

I believe we can all tune in. Some people are just extremely good at interpreting it all. They are receiving information. They use smells, colors, and symbols. I mentioned about making your own list of meanings. Your own universal language. You choose what the symbols mean to you.

I would love to see that medium again. She must have been so overwhelmed and scared as a child with no one to go to for help in understanding it. I can't imagine what it would be like if my family and people around me thought I was crazy. (Well, I think some think I'm slightly nuts). So many of these amazing people ended up in psych wards. I remember saying to her, "I think you are using more of your brain capabilities than the rest of us." I didn't really know what I meant by it at the time but I'm starting to wonder if when we truly unlock our brain potential then everything starts to flow. You are in a higher level of consciousness so it's a higher level of receiving. They just know instinctively how to connect to a particular frequency. It can be understood scientifically. Our brain is the receiver. Most of us have just blocked or muted the channels we can receive.

I don't think people should be scared anymore or thought of as crazy. I say if you think you have gifts then share them with the world. We are seeing what we can become so show your uniqueness. You may actually find yourself not so unique or alone. There are plenty of people out there that will resonate with you. All of us have known that someone is going to ring or have had a feeling about something that has come true. We see glimpses of our intuitive skills daily. They come in super handy.

I have been told that a lot of amazing adults and children can connect easily to the "Vibrational Library". It's said that often people with Autism and other abilities are truly amazing. I have heard that they are extremely connected to the Universe. This is why they are so intelligent. They are receiving more downloads than a lot of us. We do more thinking, and they do more receiving. I'm not sure if this is true, but I think there's something extra incredible about people with special abilities. Imagine being in a world where people were trying to make you different from who you really are. Would that bring you tension if others were trying to fit you into their "norm" and you really couldn't be who they think you should be? Maybe next time think about if you really need to change someone from who they truly are.

"What could you do today to move your life forward towards a new dawn?" - Sophie Howard

Let go of what you think your life needs to be. Take care of yourself. Let go enough to allow the Universe to set you up for a more incredible life. Allow life to show you how much more you can become. Just allow your heart to be open. If you can pour more love into yourself, then you're not waiting for a better world.

Can you take the opportunity to become the person you have wanted to be? Create and take the time to love yourself. Take the love and embrace your fear, anger, and frustrations. You will start to feel safer in the world and trust your intuition.

What can you do today to make your life better? Stop worrying about the past. Stop worrying about the future. Live in the now.

Small actions done with care and a pure heart every day have tremendous value and can influence the world around you, as well as the world at large.

Laugh, smile, be kind. Find love in the world. I don't mean human companion love; I mean love within yourself. Try not to judge yourself or others. Anger and frustration can cause illness so calm your mind and send love, compassion and kindness to those that frustrate you.

I've been finding now when I write a text or email or write anything on social media, I stop and I think. Is this going to make me feel good? Is this going to make the receiver feel good? Is this going to lower my own vibration and the world's vibration? What you are putting out there counts more than you think.

There are always things to do but there's only one of you.

Set Intentions

- To stay in a state of appreciation
- To be present with people you are interacting with
- Find things you enjoy
- Meditation
- To be patient with people who are on a different wavelength
- To allow yourself to rest when it is time to rest

When you are writing your intention statement, you want to focus on the positive aspects of the intention you are setting. You also want to state it in a way that is simple and repeatable easily and quickly.

There's so much more good in the world than you could ever know. The Universe is full of love and wants us all to be happy. We are the ones that are stopping ourselves from fully enjoying the wonders of this planet. Just have fun. We blame things on the outside world. *My happiness isn't dependent on the outside world.*

We are more important than we think we are. We are leading-edge creators. We are evolving and expanding our knowledge, our creations, at such a fast pace. We as a collective are seeing who we can become in such a significant way. We should be proud of ourselves for being involved in such a diverse, contrasting, confronting space. It shows such power to be in this world.

The more you struggle the harder life is. I love the analogy Abraham Hicks uses where you can either flow downstream or fight against the current and try and get upstream. Fighting against the current is exhausting and most people would drown if they did that forever. It's best to release what you can't control and just flow with the current. When your body is flowing and relaxed, you have more energy and awareness.

Do you have a soul purpose? I think we can overthink it all. I feel deep down in our hearts we all want to be happy. Success to me is happiness. For me, I feel that my soul purpose is to find what makes me happy. To align with my true self.

It's been described to me like playing the warm/hot/cold game. You're getting warmer and warmer. The happier something makes you feel the closer you are to finding your purpose. So instead of saying I'm getting warmer, you can say I'm getting happier.

You have the freedom to choose whatever you want. The only thing that is stopping you is limiting beliefs. You get taught so much from birth. "Be careful; don't do that; you failed; try harder; you lost; money doesn't grow on trees; life is hard; what are you doing with your life?"

I'm sure you could come up with plenty of things you've been taught that create limitations. What if you could just push reset? Would you wipe everything away and start fresh? I really don't think I would want to erase all the random things I've been told or all the 'dumb' things I've done in life. I definitely think the contrast helps you grow but, in the end, it doesn't define you. It can shape you and mold you, but you have the power and free will to do or be anything you want. None of those old thought patterns or beliefs really matter in the here and now.

You must give yourself time and some credit every day for trying. We can't just jump out of bed and find our purpose straight away. (Well, some people probably can but that definitely wasn't me!) My purpose is evolving as I go because I'm an eternal being. I don't want my purpose to be one thing and then that's the end.

It takes time to find pure happiness, but you can practice until you get closer and closer. It's seriously like riding a bike. You just have to keep practicing.

Nobody's perfect. How boring would that be? They say if we were all perfect and everyone liked the same thing, and the world was completely peaceful, and everyone was happy we wouldn't have the expansion or evolution that we have had here on Earth.

The goal is to know yourself. Your goal in life is not to get heaps of likes and praise. But if you enjoy that and it truly makes you happy then go for it. If it makes you feel bad about yourself and stressed then forget it.

Short term dopamine hits? Why not give your body long term happiness?

Are you listening to your own intuition and inner voice? Stop listening and looking at the external and start healing the internal. So many distractions—internet, media, the list goes on and on.

Your soul is gathered with other souls that are in the same vibration. They gather with others that are into similar things just like you do. But the souls don't have the negative thoughts and feelings like we do so as a whole they are connected as one with complete love and kindness. They understand each other. They are one consciousness connected but they have their individual loves and focus. Each one of us is a separate drop of water in a larger connected ocean.

Your soul is the best feeling part of you. Your inner guidance knows exactly how amazing you truly are. The relationship with your soul is up to you. Your soul is everything you've ever been and everything you will become.

When you feel insecure or you feel anxious, that's not your soul feeling that way. Your soul doesn't agree with you feeling bad. It's pure positive energy. It's trying to show you and guide you all the way. It doesn't feel stressed or frustrated. It's soothing, loving energy. It doesn't judge you or blame you or feel you are doing things wrong. You are the one that feels you're doing things wrong sometimes. It's your analytical mind.

When you're having an amazing day and you are totally tuned in, you're in alignment. Everything's going right. You're appreciating life. You're buzzing and tingling. That's when you can really feel your soul. That's you, but it's just the version of you that doesn't have any resistance.

It lets go of the struggles. I hear people say their "soul is tired" but I don't really believe that. The soul is plugged into the Universe that creates worlds. The source of life is powerful positive pure energy. That's what your soul is. The part of you that is tired is your mind and your body, not your soul. The body gets tired when you're not connecting and looking after yourself. The mind gets tired from over-analyzing, overthinking, and overcompensating.

You have so much power you can connect to. The source of the Universe is flowing through you. People think they are so limited, but they aren't. Scientists are discovering more and more about the energy that surrounds us. Breathe it in. Connect with it and realize your full potential.

It's ok where you are right now. You're not wrong. It's not your fault. You have done a great job navigating this space and time. You are learning so much on your journey.

If you want to be perfect just be yourself.

Universal forces are focused on you. They are here to support and guide you. They are not looking at you thinking that you are doing everything completely wrong. What you think is wrong is completely right because every single thing we do expands the Universe. We are exploring and creating. We are seeing the good and the bad. So all of the good stuff from Earth is waiting for us. It's hard to understand this if you're stuck in the earth grid. So you're just in your own earth bubble being distracted and overwhelmed by what's in front of you.

What dimension / density are you in?

Do you ever hear about vortex's, dimensions, density's or multiverses? Are there other dimensions? Some liken it to *Alice in Wonderland* and *The Wizard of Oz*. How did Alice get to her Wonderland? Obviously these are books and movies but it kind of gives you a picture of other realms. How exactly did Dorothy get transported to Oz? Where did that portal come from that delivered Alice to her Wonderland? The tales do have something in common. Dorothy's tornado and Alice's doorway to wonderland are both vortexes. We know the storylines of The Wizard of Oz and Alice in Wonderland are born from fiction, but does the same hold true for the vortex? Are they there but we can't see them with our limited spectrum?

At this present day it is not known how many dimension levels in our universe can be observed or detected by humans. The total is assumed to be infinite, but it is likely we can only find a limited number of them. A limited number within a limited range have been found and classified, but there are way more vortices that are still waiting to be discovered.

Spiritual vortexes are said to be cross-points between energy fields in the earth's grid system, or intersecting ley lines. Where the ley lines intersect, in certain areas, the result is said to be a "hot spot" of energy.

Much the same way that we drive our cars along highways, it has also been suggested that vortexes can be portals into other realms, much like Alice's Wonderland or Dorothy's Oz. To some, these vortexes are doorways into other dimensions. This type of vortex is where it's said that swirling masses of electromagnetic energy come to the surface, similar to the way lava is expelled from a volcano. It is also described that dimensions are merely densities. So depending on what frequency or vibration you are on will depend on what you feel, see and hear.

The chakra system is believed to consist of mini personal vortexes in the human body—energy centers that power our life force.

A large number of people believe that we have a vibrational vortex. It's a vibrational environment with everything we've ever dreamed of. This is where we have come from. So when we pass we go to this pure positive energy vortex, dimension, realm. Some call it heaven. We come to earth for the contrast and the resistance so we can expand our consciousness and find what we truly love and what really makes us happy. When we transition back, we leave the stress and the physical pain, but we have learned so much from being here in this beautiful contrasting world.

So many people are saying now that death is nothing to be afraid of because there is no death. When you transition you release your body and don't even miss it because it's not your true essence. Who you truly are is a magnificent being/soul/ higher power.

It's said we are in a three-dimensional world. We have length, width and depth-and one dimension of time. String theory states that the Universe operates in 10 dimensions but there's the mind blowing possibility that far more exist. Our souls, higher self, inner being, whatever you like to call it is always there with you. Some people say "I have no soul" when they do something wrong. That's not true at all. Your soul is always there with strength and power, appreciating you and loving you nonstop no matter what you do. It's your guidance—your life force. It gives you energy, knowledge, and wisdom. It is you. It's flowing through you right now as you're reading this book.

Laws Of The Universe

Matias De Stefano describes that there is a law of the Universe but in order for us humans to understand it the law is split into seven laws. The laws are split between our seven energy points. Some call them the seven chakras. Our chakras are bounded to the laws of the Universe. Personally I've heard we have more than seven energy points but maybe he's talking about the main ones?

Matias believes that the laws of the Universe affect us. He believes that the laws keep the whole entire Universe in order. Kind of like we have laws on earth. The Universe has its own set of laws. It doesn't matter what time or space you are in or what you create in the Universe you are still part of the "Universal Laws." You are creating and expanding the Universe. In this planet we are on the planet of the third dimension. As humans we find it hard to understand the laws of the Universe. In ancient times we were taught these laws but over time we have lost our understanding of them.

The laws are within us. Our whole body.

You can be an alchemist, a creator of your own reality. The seventh dimension they say is the one of enlightenment, where everyone is so well. Some people call it heaven. "Seventh Heaven." It's the place where you can see and feel everything, in a good way. It has so much light and clarity. You are not in need of creating.

In the seventh dimension people are so coherent they just dream about realities. So pretty much it's all of your best dreams come true. You can be or do whatever you please. It feels like someone that has accomplished everything. You can feel every possibility of who you can be. You just have to think about it and then you can be it. Everything you're thinking, your thoughts become real. It materializes in front of you.

Matias believes there are seven main laws of the Universe:

Crown Chakra—Mentalism:

Everything you live is what you believe. You must change the way you move the energy through your mind and become what you want. You create the reality when you feel it. We are imperfect otherwise we wouldn't experience anything. Our world is imperfect so that we learn, grow, and expand. Perfection doesn't get us anywhere. We wouldn't move forward.

Third Eye—Correspondence:

You can see who you really are from within. We can see the positive and the negative of ourselves. This helps us to see our reality. Everything comes from the mind. Everything is connected by vibration.

Throat Chakra—Vibration:

The throat chakra makes the vibration. Low vibrations attract low vibrations and high vibrations make higher vibrations. What you say is what you're going to create. Be careful what you think and how you say things. It all comes back to you.

Heart Chakra—Rhythm:

You are positive and negative. You have different rhythms in creation. If your vibration is low, the time will seem longer. If you're in a higher vibration, you can get what you want faster. If you change the way you talk and think then you bring more positive things in. Slow down and have time to think about what you're saying.

Solar plexus—Cause and effect:

It's conditioning everything that's happening in your life. Whatever you do affects your life. Nothing just happens; there's always a reason. You can start to understand why things are happening to you. We can't blame others for things that happen to us. If you're vibrating very low, then something can happen to you, so you experience it to show you how low you are feeling. That's why bad things happen to good people. You need to try and vibrate higher. Lift your mood and your way of thinking.

Sacral Chakra—Polarity:

This helps you go from one point to another. We are electrons, protons, neutrons. Positive and negative makes us exist. Good and bad is a way to evolve and go forward. Everything that creates us is magnetic. The only way you can go up is from going down and you take the energy to jump up again. You can't jump higher if you don't bend down first. So that's why we have ups and downs. Polarity helps us to move forward.

Root Chakra—Generation:

Positive or negative is generating everything. Nothing ever dies. It just keeps transforming itself. We are creating new realities at every second.

Some believe there are more than seven laws. It's up to you to decide what resonates with you. The list goes on. There are a few more added below. Which ones are you drawn to?

The Law of Divine Oneness - The Law of Divine Oneness is the foundational law, stating that everything is connected.

The Law of Vibration - Every particle in the Universe is constantly moving and carries energy.

The Law of Correspondence - Patterns repeat throughout the Universe.

Law Of Attraction - Like attracts like. In order to work out what you want you need to vibrate on the same frequency as it. Pessimism or fear will lead you to generate more negative experiences.

Law of Inspired Action - Actively pursue your goals when you get an inspiration from your guidance.

Law of Perpetual Transmutation of Energy - Everything around us is in constant flux. Some of them are on a cellular or atomic level. Higher vibrations can help bring lower vibrations up.

The Law of Cause and Effect - Actions have corresponding reactions. Sometimes people say this is where Karma comes into it.

The Law of Compensation - You receive what you put out there. It reminds us to be careful how we treat others.

The Law of Relativity - There are multiple perspectives. Nothing is good or bad until you compare it to something else. You might not feel poor until you see someone else with more. It can show you how to make improvements in your life.

The Law of Polarity - Everything has an opposite. That's how we understand life. When you have hard times, it makes you appreciate the good times.

The Law of Rhythm - Everything comes in cycles. Perpetual movement. It can prepare you for the next thing.

The Law of Gender - There are two main energy types. Masculine and Feminine. Yin and Yang. We all contain an energy of both. Some have more of one than the other.

The Law of Reflectivity - Meaning that anywhere in the Universe information can be sent and received. The base of its structure is geometry. It is reflected in any part of the earth, galaxy, Universe, or Multiverse.

(Inspired from articles on the website - thelawofattraction.com and Caroline Cory workshops - omniumuniverse.com and videos from - gaia.com)

Are you coherent with the laws? What do you think about yourself? What do you feel within? Is it what you see outside of yourself?

Think about what your vibration is in this Universe. Are you balanced? Do you respect yourself and your life? What do you feel and what do you love? Are you causing anything that affects you in your life? Ask yourself how you feel.

Whatever fights against us can give us another perspective of who we are. If you're fighting against something, then someone else is probably fighting against you. Polarity helps us to go forward.

Emotionally, mentally, and physically we are creators. We cannot blame anyone else for our lives. We are in charge of creating it. We all have freedom. We have the freedom to decide for ourselves.

Are You Conscious?

How awake are you really? There's so much talk of consciousness. Are you conscious or are you just living day to day going around in circles on this planet we call Earth? Are you actually awake? Or are you just stuck in a repeating pattern living day to day? Working to make money. Eating, Sleeping. Repeating. It can take time to get behind the analytical mind. There are programs and beliefs we have since birth. There are earth grids, different frequencies interrupting our frontal cortex. Some liken the matrix movie to us when we are stuck in limiting belief systems. We are on autopilot repeating old habits. Not realizing that there is so much more out there. This world is like a fun game and our bodies are the avatars. It's a frill ride for souls.

I feel like I was stuck in a globe or a bubble. You can tap into the amazing resources of the Universe. It's all there, waiting for you to break through the globe and see what you can truly become. Your potential is indescribable. It's so incredible that there aren't words big enough to say how amazing you are. Mind over matter. Have you ever wondered why those people can karate chop blocks and pieces of wood with their bare hands? They believe they can. They know that everything is energy, and they tell themselves that they can do it. I mean people can walk through fire and be totally fine. It's all in your belief system.

I really wouldn't get caught up with the world's drama, what your family thinks or what you think is true. Who really knows what is true?

A phenomenon I love to explore is the *Mandela* effect.

This is a very interesting occurrence. It's where people believe they have heard or seen something at some point in time, but if you try and find that information now it's changed. It started with people believing that Nelson Mandela died in prison, but he actually passed years later. People have heard of other people passing but suddenly, they are alive. There are names of books that have changed. Cartoon characters or quotes are different.

Did a dimensional shift occur, and some people remember, and some don't? Did a time/space anomaly happen? Did angels or universal architects change history? One theory originates from quantum physics and relates to the idea that rather than one timeline there is a possibility of alternate realities or multiverses taking place on our timeline. Are they just false memories that a large collective of people have? One person might have said a "fact" onthe Internet so everyone thinks it's true. For fun Google the "Mandela Effect examples."

"The Mandela Effect is a phenomenon in which a person or a group of people have false or distorted memories. Some believe that the Mandela Effect is proof of alternate realities, while others blame it on the fallibility of human memory." - Medical News today. (medicalnewstoday.com)

The reality gets changed. It can happen personally or globally. They call them false memories but that's how we remember it.

The heart used to be more on the left but now it's more in the middle. The kidneys were lower but now they are higher so the ribs can protect them. Do you remember the old fairy tale, "Mirror mirror on the wall who's the fairest of them all"? Or was it "Magic mirror on the wall who's the fairest of them all"? Was it "Luke, I am your father"? In fact, it was, "No, I am your father." Even the actor that said the lines remembers saying it the first way. So many sayings or quotes or images suddenly change. This is the "Mandela Effect."

The golden timeline is an idea that there's a choice we can make to stay open and connected and receive information and dreams no matter what is going on around us. The timeline can change and there are many possibilities and opportunities. We are capable of being anything we want. You are part of the consciousness of the Universe.

Listen to the answers that come from within. What is your self-worth actually tied to? Is it how much you have or how you feel? If you feel abundant, you will have abundance. If you feel happy you will be happy. You don't need something huge to make you happy.

"BEAUTY IS NOT IN THE FACE: BEAUTY IS A LIGHT IN THE HEART"

KAHIL GIBRAN

CHAPTER 7

WHAT MAKES YOU HAPPY?

"We have to be happy in order to get what we want instead of the other way around. If you want to see a change in the world, then be happy and make other people happy."

- DEEPAK CHOPRA

It's not someone else's responsibility to make you happy. You can't steal the happiness of others. You need to be able to help yourself before helping others. Emotions will drain you. Recovery time can be days and weeks. We are all unique individuals. Find things that work for you. Start doing things for yourself. Children and adults don't benefit from you doing everything for them all the time. Focus on yourself.

Be inspired rather than sick and tired. Meaning you don't want to wait until you get an illness or injury. To me it would be way more fun to become inspired rather than letting yourself get exhausted trying to do everything.

Vibrational Frequency

Life is kind of confusing but just do your best. You will get influenced in so many ways. From advertising to someone telling you about their latest diet to what you should put on your skin.

Just don't stress and worry that you shouldn't have eaten something, or you should have tried something else. It's good to be mindful about the food we are eating and the products we are using. So much of it these days isn't that great for our bodies. (If you wouldn't drink it then why would you put it on your skin which is a living organ?)

I'm loving how so many creators and producers are trying to develop new healthier products. We can find what's good for our bodies but if we overthink it, then we just put a stigma on it and our minds tell us it's bad so our bodies can react. If you worry too much about food and products, then you're telling your body that it could be something negative. We are essentially energy so I don't think it should matter what we eat but our human perspective tells us otherwise.

Your body is part of your vibrational frequency so it's great to look after it as much as you can. It does make a difference when you start to really connect to your body. Exercise and eating healthy food can keep your body vibrating high but don't overthink it all as well. We are here to enjoy all of the flavors of the earth.

Exercise can be very beneficial and can help your body release any stuck energies. It can really help release stress. I think doing something physical for at least fifteen minutes a day can really make a difference.

I really don't like being told what to do. I'm not into diets. I just think if it makes you feel good go for it but if it makes you feel stressed or unwell, then it's not so good. I still love the old saying "80/20." I try to be healthy 80 percent of the time, whatever that means, and the other 20 percent I'll have what people would call a treat.

I highly recommend taking time for yourself. Yoga, walking, anything you enjoy.

It was recommended to me to eat a rainbow of foods. Non processed. Limit alcohol as it can inflame the body. Ground with the earth. Don't overdo the exercise every day as it can put your body into a fight, flight or freeze mode and store fat. Obviously, it's up to you. If you are in tune with your body, you should recognize if something is making you feel more stressed or if it's making you feel happier. If you don't feel good, then maybe consider finding things that make you feel better. It's all trial and error.

What feels best to you moment to moment? Focus on that.

Personally, I think it's best not to overthink it. It's all in your perception. Keep it simple. If you think something is going to make you overweight, then that's what you are telling your body. It also depends on how you're feeling. If you just want to eat or drink to drown your sorrows, then it's probably going to affect you more. If you're just having food or a drink as a celebration, and you're feeling good within yourself then it seems more logical that you would still feel happy and healthy.

Again, I'm not a healthcare professional, scientist or have actual proof so I would seek advice if you are concerned about your consumption or wellbeing in any area. There are some amazing helpful nutritionists and people out there with great ideas. When you learn to connect with your mind again, then you will start to get the right people to come in with ideas on how to help you. Just make sure you pick someone when you are feeling good. If you choose your practitioner out of desperation, you might not find the right person. You'll just find someone that's in that same vibration. It's like being on the same wavelength with someone. You want them to be the right fit and get you.

"Raising Your Frequency with Essential Oils"
Kate from ORA (Ordinary Rituals Aromatherapy) talks about frequency.

"I know I am not the only one feeling especially sensitive to the energies buzzing about these days. We know there is a lot of heaviness happening in our own world and the greater world around us.

"Some of you may be new to the concept of understanding our energy, and how to 'raise your frequency' it might sound like a little bit of hippie hoo ha, but perhaps you are open to understanding it more?

"Remember back in science class when you were 13 or so, we learned how EVERYTHING is energy? - everything is made up of molecules - moving molecules - so even something solid like your chair, is actually countless molecules vibrating with life and frequency!

"So with that in mind, we can begin to understand more of how the universe works. It is a lot easier to play a part when we think in terms of vibration (and energy). Think of frequencies - like a radio, tuning in to different frequencies via radio waves will allow you to tune into different channels. Our bodies too are impacted by different things we come into contact with which can change our own frequencies!

"Typically, our bodies run around at different frequencies. Everything we touch and eat has frequencies which can affect us—e.g. food—processed food can measure lower in frequency, whereas fresh food, fruit or veg can have higher measurements. But also, our thinking can affect our frequency. "If you have negative thoughts, it can lower your frequency but positive thoughts can raise your frequency.

"Essential Oils run at different frequencies.- Essential oils can run at high frequencies. No wonder they make us feel so good right?!

"Your body attunes to its surroundings, so if you surround yourself with positive frequencies like essential oils, happy things, people who make you feel good, cats, animals, trees, oceans! then you will be able to lift your body frequency.

"Thank you for raising the vibration of our planet with your choice to lift it with your positivity."

Kate xx https://oraaromatherapy.com/

Crystals Are My Candy

"It is the life of the crystal, the architect of the flake, the fire of the frost, the soul of the sunbeam. This crisp winter air is full of it." - John Burroughs

A number of people lately have found that crystals make them happy. We see crystals every day in the form of salt, sugar, gemstones, and snowflakes. Crystals are prized for their beauty in gemstones and valued for their utility in many electronic products. Some people believe crystals have spiritual and healing qualities, as well. There orderly, repeating patterns are a marvel of nature and chemistry.

I have to give a shout out to my crystals for helping me feel good. I'm not saying that they do have healing properties, but I do believe there is definitely something special to them. We started a crystal boutique store in New Zealand just for fun. I was reading a *Vogue* article about crystals being a trend and a lot of celebs were right into it, so I thought why not sell a few to family and friends? Social media got busy, and everyone was asking how to buy them, so I created my website. lilyleaf11.com

Lilyleaf was named after the lotus flower and water lilies that are one of my favorite flowers. After having the crystals around me I realized that a lot of amazing things were happening. I had more clarity. I had a better feeling about myself. There was contentment flowing through me. I just realized I had found something that made me happy in a roundabout way.

I read an article, which led me to buy a basket of crystals, which led me to create social media pages, which led me to create an online boutique, which led me to write a book. It just flowed. All of these little signs and options were there for me to take. I realized the Universe was sending me what I wanted, but I didn't know exactly what I had wanted at the beginning. I kind of wanted to have a store but I had no idea where to start. No business skills at all. The Universe guided me all of the way. I just had to relax and recognize the signs. I could tell by my gut feeling. It felt right.

You don't have to wander around in silk robes burning sage with crystals tied to your head to find the power within. But it is kind of fun.

To Crystal Cleanse or Not to Cleanse

Should I cleanse my crystals? I say just go with your intuition. Crystals have been used for centuries for energy usage and have been used in TVs, radios and cell phones. They can amplify and have storage capabilities. Some people like to cleanse their crystals because over the years crystals have stored memory. That's why they use them in computers. It's hard to know what memories or energies are stored in the crystals. I like to just set an intention that my crystals are full of life, love, and positivity. You can cleanse them under a full moon. Some say bury or put in salt but that's not what I'm into. I wouldn't want them to get damaged. It does totally depend on the crystal because some of them are very tough and sturdy. We broke three drill pieces trying to make incense holders out of rose quartz.

It's been said you can wash your crystals in water. I did a lot of this at the beginning because it looked great on my Lilyleaf11 Instagram page but then I realized I needed to be more careful because a number of crystals are very fragile so it's best to double check they are not going to disintegrate in the water. Another good one to check is sunlight. Some crystal colors can fade when exposed to the sun so just double check. A few crystals these days have also been colored to make the markings stand out, and it creates a brighter look. Often, they dye agate a brighter color for fun. You must be careful as the dye fades in the sun and can leach out onto your surface especially if it gets wet. Just tap into your heart and see what's right for you.

Crystal Cleanse

(Free PDF Available on Lilyleaf11.com)

Crystal Cleanse

A guide to cleansing crystals and crystal properties.

lilyleaf11.com

To Cleanse or not to cleanse.

Cleanse your crystals as often as you need to. I think you can just hold a crystal and if you feel it needs a little cleanse then go for it but if you think it's fine then leave it. Just ask your heart and trust your gut. They do store a lot of memory so that's why people often like to cleanse them. Don't overthink it all.

Full Moon
The Moon reflects the light of the sun. Lay your crystals on the window sill and bathe your crystals in the moon's photons. Apparently, this recharges the crystals and the energy rubs off on us. They can help you tap into your inner strength.

Moon Energy
You might not always want to wait for the full moon if you use your crystals often. You can also work with moon energies. As a way to charge your stones and give them a soft and gentle boost of a beautiful calming feminine energy.

Sunlight
This can have celestial light energy. Sunshine is strong and vibrant. It strengthens. You do need to double-check if your crystals can handle the sun. For example, some crystals can lose their color and become clear.

Water
If you don't have time to cleanse in other ways you can use tap water. It's not a deep cleanse but it will help if you're in a rush. Apparently, living water is a powerful way to cleanse. So rivers, waterfalls, lakes and the ocean. Any water that comes directly from Mother Earth. Gently lapping waves are beautiful, but if it's seawater remember to check if the crystals are ok with salt.

Smudging
In addition to their medicinal healing properties, plants have high vibrational properties. Sage, sweetgrass or palo santo, cedar and juniper are all great. When you smudge you light the plant but you don't need heaps of smoke. You can just let it slowly burn.

Incense
Create a sacred space. The smoke from the incense can clear the energetic frequencies. The fragrance can be healing. It can energetically and emotionally impact you.

Eclipses

Solar and lunar eclipses have been said to have a powerful energy that helps you change things in your life if you're feeling stagnant. Put your crystals out on the window sill over this time to give them an extra boost.

Buried in the earth

Sometimes a stone can be so energetically heavy. You can bury the stone in mother earth or you can place it in a box. Check again that your stone can handle the dirt if you are putting it straight into it without protecting the crystal. Some don't like to get dirty or wet.

Salt

Mother earth's salt can hold powerful energies. I would protect your crystals if I was putting them into salt. All life on earth began in the salty water billions of years ago. It has supercharged energy even if it's not in the water anymore.

Visualisation

Some say you can visualise a white light flowing through the crystals. This can take a bit of practice. It's like your sending the crystals your good vibes. You can use mental imagery to create your desire.

Candle flame

You can set an intention with a candle flame. Put your crystals nearby but obviously don't leave your candle unattended. It's fun to watch the flame and relax into the subtle energy.

Sound

You can use music. Sound bowls. Gongs. Sound and vibrational healing is a great tool. A single pitch or tone can wash over the crystal and cleanse the energies.

There are also crystals that don't need cleansing. Some crystals have a higher vibration like selenite. So the natural divine energy flows through it more than some other crystals. You can also use selenite to cleanse your other crystals.

Caution
Not all crystals are physically capable of being buried in dirt or being left outside. Being in direct sunlight or having the capability for water cleanse. Please double check first. There's plenty of great info on the internet these days. Don't leave your flames unattended.

Some common Crystal & Stone properties

Agate *Soothes Negativity x Calm x Peace*

Angel Aura *Faith x Positivity x Bonds*

Amazonite *Calm x Soothe x Balance*

Amethyst *Healing x Power x Protect*

Ametrine *Balance x Acceptance x Calm*

Amber *Wisdom x Patience x Balance*

Aragonite *Stabilising x Stress relief x Grounding*

Apophyllite *Negativity x Happiness x Peace*

Aquamarine *Creativity x Self Expression x Clarity*

Aventurine *Soothing x Abundance x Calm*

Bismuth *Calm x Focus x Individualisation*

Black Obsidian *Grounds x Protects x Mind*

Black Tourmaline *Communication x Inspiration x Creativity*

Bloodstone *Courage x Motivation x Creative Energy*

Calcite *Higher Consciousness x Connects emotions*

Carnelian *Clarity x Peace x Courage*

Chalcopyrite *Cleansing x Aligning x Balancing*

Copper *Energy flow x Balance x Motivation*

Clear Quartz *Energy x Clarity x Healing*

Citrine *Clarity x Prosperity x Optimism x Abundance*

Chrysocolla *Calm x Cleanse x Re-energise*

Chrysoprase *New love x Abundance x Prosperity*

Celestite *Calming x Uplifting x Emotional wellbeing*

Desert Rose *Healing x Regeneration x Nausea*

Diamond *Courage x Energy x Self Esteem*

Emerald *Inspiration x Soothing x Healing*

Fluorite *Confidence x Protective x Wealth*

Fuchsite *Heals Trauma x Positivity x Release Blockages*

Galena *Compassion x Love x Tolerance*

Garnet *Balance x Passion x Inspires*

Gold *Balance x Confidence x Energy fields*

Herkimer *High Vibration x Master Healer x Energy Blocks*

Howlite *Memory x Patience x Calming*

Jade *Peace x Wisdom x Balance*

Jasper *Endurance x Balance x Stability*

Kyanite *Meditation x Attunement x Calm*

Labradorite *Good energy x Protection x Positive change*

Lapis lazuli *Protection x Peace x Harmony*

Larimar *Healing x Wisdom x Love*

Lepidolite *Anxiety x Peace x Harmony*

Malachite *Endurance x Inner peace x Sleep*

Moonstone *New beginnings x Hope x Strength*

Moldavite *Energy x Transformation x Can cause tingling*

Morganite *Stress x Oxygen flow x Heart healing*

Ocean *Jasper Stillness x Strength x Purification*

Opal *Love x Peace x Consciousness*

Opalite *Curiosity x Optimism x Negativity*

Onyx *Focus x Strength x Protection*

Peacock *Ore Happiness x Joy x Upliftment*

Pink Opal *Love x Peace x Hope*

Pyrite *Wealth x Warmth x Prosperity*

Quartz *Master Healer x Harmony x Clarity*

Rhodonite *Compassion x Balance x Love*

Rhodochrosite *Love x Passion x Soul energise*

Ruby Fuchsite *Positivity x Individuality x Connection*

Ruby Zoisite *Courage x Strength x Fear*

Rose Quartz *Calm x Peace x Love*

Selenite *Peace x Calm x Meditation*

Silver *Balance x Clarity x Harmony*

Smoky Quartz *Clarity x Positivity x Calm*

Sodalite *Calmness x Truth x Balance*

Super Six *Healing x Intuition x Knowledge*

Tigers Eye *Reduces fear + anxiety x Balance*

Topaz *Energy x Relaxation x Creativity*

Tourmaline *Compassion x Tolerance x Prosperity*

Turquoise *Purification x Protection x Wisdom*

Unakite *Love x Compassion x Kindness*

Zoisite *Intuitive x Anger x Emotional body healer*

What to pick

I think you should definitely ask your intuition. Sometimes it's good to feel what color you are drawn to at the time or not even the color just the crystal. People always ask me what is the best Crystal for... an example would be 'love'. Rose Quartz is a well-known crystal for love. It's the Universal Stone of love but I wouldn't necessarily say to get Rose Quartz if you want love because you might have a block somewhere else in your body that needs clearing. You may need a completely different stone before love can come into your life so just trust your gut and go with the one that is calling to you. It should pop and give you a good feeling when you see it.

lilyleaf11.com
@lilyleaf11

Earthing

I've found when you are happy it's easier to figure things out because you can see the right options for you. If you're stressed, then that's the energy you're drawing in, so the path gets a bit bumpier. It's like going off-roading. You're close to the right road, but you've just taken the harder route.

Can you find what makes you happy? For me I like yoga and meditation. I've been wanting to try Tai Chi. Maybe one day. I also enjoy Body Combat and dance classes at the gym. I love watching surfing and hanging out at the beach. I think it's so beneficial to connect with nature and there is a lot of scientific evidence and grounding physics now about the connection between the body and grounding on the earth. The theory is that like the powerlines we have electricity and grounding affects the living matrix which is the connector between our living cells.

The benefits and importance of "Earthing" yourself is being scientifically discovered. Touch the bare earth. Walk along the beach. Take your shoes off on the grass. I have seen a documentary where a physician talks about how her baby was always upset and as soon as she put the baby outside on the earth the baby would be so happy. They say it can help the body with inflammation and other ailments. As we have evolved we have forgotten to get back to nature. We wear shoes all day. We stay indoors more. A lot of people don't get to experience the beauty of nature and have forgotten its importance to our cycle of life. What do you do to ground yourself and get back out into nature?

Be deliberate in what you are doing. Don't try to control the conditions or circumstances. You can't be happy if you try to control everyone or everything around you. Just try and feel a little better each day.

It's hard if you're sick, have a disease or injury. It can start to consume you and you start focusing on it the whole time. You must trust and believe that your body can heal. You just need to tune yourself in and find what's best for you. If you tune into your guidance system, it might find the right doctor or the right healthcare professionals or healing specialists.

Tension is putting resistance on the things you really want. You can still receive what you want being stressed and unhappy but it's so much more fun letting go of all resistance and focusing on happiness.

Stop. Slow down. Take a few breaths and see if you feel a little bit better. Reach for thoughts that make you feel at ease. Find more good feeling thoughts. The more you practice feeling good the faster you can come back to feeling better.

Take your attention off the hard topics. Sometimes it's hard to fight against the bigger things. Just try and find a subject that feels better.

Don't try and figure out what anyone is doing or what anyone needs. Everyone has their own experiences on earth.

Let everyone around you and everyone you love be their own person. Let them live their lives. It's their journey and their soul plan. Focus on yourself and feeling good. You can't rely on anyone else to make you feel good.

Raise Your Home's Energy

Declutter: Let the energy flow easily rather than having too much stuff for it to get through. Clear clutter for clarity.

Clean: Use natural products. You can even add crystals and essential oils to your cleaning products for extra good vibes. I just use a bit of white vinegar and water in a glass spray bottle with rose quartz for love or citrine for wealth. I also use a vanilla essence and water mix with crystals to get rid of any unwanted smells.

Flowers: Fresh flowers from the garden or dried flowers if you don't like changing the water. Bring nature inside.

Plants: One of my favorites. They provide extra oxygen. Take in carbon dioxide. Improve your mood. Reduce fatigue, boost healing and pain tolerance. Lower anxiety. Ease dry skin and respiratory ailments due to dry air.

Crystals: These can definitely raise the frequency of the home or office space. They protect, lift, revive.

Windows: Open often to release old stagnant energies. I love a fresh house full of clean new air.

Candles: Light to create ambience. They can be calming and relaxing. You can use them while making your intentions. Focus on the good things you want to bring into your life.

If you like you can write a list of what makes you happy. What makes you feel good? If it doesn't make me happy then I don't do it. Obviously, there are some things that you might have to do that you really don't want to do like work but eventually when you practice feeling good then the right job will come which won't feel like real work most of the time.

What makes me feel good

☆

"YOU YOURSELF
AS MUCH AS
ANYBODY IN THE
ENTIRE UNIVERSE,
DESERVE YOUR
LOVE AND
AFFECTION".
BUDDHA

CHAPTER 8

JUST FEEL GOOD

"To be beautiful means to be yourself. You don't need to be accepted by others. You need to accept yourself."

— THICH NHAT HANH

Happiness is not something that comes to us externally. Come back to the breath and remember each moment is precious, full of potential and is yours to enjoy. You can choose to be happy. Anytime you need to remember the feeling of happiness, make contact with that place in your body that holds the energy.

By now you probably would have been told that we are often in a fight-flight or freeze "survival" mode where our instincts tell us that we are in danger. It's happening more often than not these days, through busy lifestyles, stress, and commitments. Just the thought of getting somewhere on time can put you into survival mode.

The outcome of life is the journey of life. Life has its challenges, but that's what makes it interesting. We don't want to be at our destination or be in complete control because we would lose our dreams and purpose. The outcome is the present moment so you can change it instantaneously.

The control is all yours. You can choose to be positive and choose to be happy. You can choose to be healthy. Top athletes use visualization techniques. You can visualize the life you want. Visualize yourself being happy and healthy.

"The purpose of our lives is to be happy." - Dalai Lama

Don't let conditions confine you. Be free. Be who you are. Don't go looking for the rest of society to agree with you on who you want to be. Pushing against something only makes things harder. You don't need to please everyone else or wait for everyone else to please you.

Sometimes you come across people that may not be kind. There's also a lot of people in this world that have done some not so nice things. I don't believe people's souls are bad. I just believe some human beings have been misled, mistreated, misunderstood, miseducated, and unloved. They need education, support, love, and kindness. Compassion is the key.

People think they have to prove their worth. We do not realize just how powerful we really are. We are super creators.

A Little Drop of Mindfulness

"Life gives you plenty of time to do whatever you want to do if you stay in the present moment." - Deepak Chopra

Mindfulness means maintaining a moment-by-moment awareness of our thoughts, feelings, bodily sensations, and surrounding environment, through a gentle, nurturing lens. When we practice mindfulness, our thoughts tune into what we're sensing in the present moment rather than rehashing the past or imagining the future.

"Don't let yesterday take up too much of today." – Will Rogers

Use tools to check in with yourself. How's your breathing? Such an important part of life is your breathing. I used to be a terrible breather before yoga and meditation. I used to get dizzy, tingling, numb face, heart palpitations, all because I wasn't breathing properly. Running around trying to achieve everything but not actually achieving as much as I do now with meditating and exercise, owning businesses and having kids. I was shallow breathing and not taking in oxygen in the blood. It can affect your clarity. It can give you anxiety. It can make you feel tired. The breath is the life force. It takes practice to get this flowing naturally.

We practice our breathwork at yoga and through meditation but there are breathing clinics in different areas of the country. I had to put a wheat bag on my chest and watch the wheat bag move up and down. I definitely wasn't belly breathing and often during my day I still don't breathe correctly. I'm far from perfect. It's good to practice.

There are heaps of apps and things you can get to help you with your breathing. Mindfulness apps are helpful as well.

Contrast will inspire inner desire.

Try to be more aware of things that are making you feel unwell. For example, if you've been drinking alcohol all night and you start vomiting it's your body trying to get it out of your system. Are there foods that you notice might make you feel sluggish or nauseous or upset your stomach? I'm not a nutritionist or health worker so I would get advice if you're unsure. I just like to use my intuition to figure a few steps out first. Then you can discover the right road for you.

Belief systems and blocks can make allergies worse.

"The joy of life comes from our encounters with new experiences, and hence there is no greater joy than to have an endlessly changing horizon, for each day to have a new and different sun." - Christopher McCandless

Are you appreciating food? Being pure positive energy over on the other side sounds like absolute bliss but don't you think we are incredibly lucky to be able to taste food? Smelling it, hearing it, seeing it. I do recommend "mindful" eating. This is where you stop, sit down and really take in the food experience. Take a bite and really taste it. Let your food digest while you're sitting comfortably. If you're eating on the go or not focusing, your mind doesn't always recognize you've eaten so you're still hungry.

We need a balance of Yin and Yang so some nice calm exercise as well as cardio, yoga, walking, Tai Chi and other exercises, whatever you're into. Group fitness, running, sports, etc.

Do you lay down in the grass and stare up at the clouds? I did it more as a kid. Why do we lose interest in the little moments? Are we just so overstimulated that we don't even see what's in front of our eyes? Try and focus more on what you are up to rather than what everyone else is doing.

Try not to feel sorry for people all the time. By putting out the energy that people can't fend for themselves or that they can't cope with life, you are only telling them that they are not worthy or capable. It's better to encourage people, be supportive. Show compassion. If you are sad, worried, or frustrated with them then that is the frequency you're putting out there. You're not just sending that energy to them' you're sending it to yourself and the rest of the world.

A thought attaches to a thought to another thought.

We need to start by taking note of our thoughts. What are they telling us? Do they serve us? Do they need to be there?

Are you thinking about something that happened eight months ago? Who cares! Use it as wisdom and move on. The only time now is the present so take charge of your own mind and body.

Be the creator of your world. Don't worry about what everyone else is doing and start enjoying what you're doing. Keep it simple. Once you start thinking about something you will find another thought will come in that's similar and then another and then you're away on a tangent thinking about things that don't even matter.

It's counterproductive to be out on the streets protesting for peace. We need to start thriving and stop just surviving. People have learned characteristics that make people want war, but it doesn't have to be that way.

We're not living from wishes and desires; we're living from our programs. From school, parents, government, religions, etc. Things that we have been taught since we were children. A lot of us have lost respect for each other, for cultures, and for society. Instead of coming together, we have become competitive, thinking we have to climb on top of someone to get what we want and to be the best. To me, I feel it would be amazing to come together and support each other. Lift each other up. Work together to create an even more beautiful magical world. You can achieve so much more when you're not fighting against something.

We need to remember what we are and where we have come from.

You can let go of negativity, but you won't be letting go of who you are. You will feel safe and free. It all starts with you. We can't get inside everyone else's heads, but we can start with ourselves and be role models to others. You can't have peace in the world if you're fighting with your neighbors.

There is no love and sense of belonging if there's no happiness. We are naturally wired to be happy, but we are so caught up in what we don't have instead of what we do have.

Mindfulness

"Your emotions are a processing system." - Caroline Cory

One of the big keys to success in life is mindfulness. A mindful life can be tranquil, joyful, blissful, ecstatic, and compassionate. Through mindfulness, we can establish a direct connection to the Universe. It is the solution that we have sought externally as human beings since the dawn of modernity. Even though mindfulness has been practiced for thousands of years, most people prefer more complex and intellectual philosophies or techniques. This outward journey never concludes. Numerous individuals and texts complicate and over-analyze mindfulness. Our minds seem to be wired in such a way that even the simplest solutions become complicated.

Mindfulness is meant to be an uncomplicated yet profound way of life. This solution, which is centered on the present moment, enables us to live authentic lives. Therefore, what is mindfulness, and how do you integrate it into your daily life?

Mindfulness is a type of meditation that focuses on present-moment awareness. There are numerous types of meditation; however, mindfulness is one that is believed to be the most practical meditation. Mindfulness entails actively participating in each moment as it unfolds while remaining fully aware of your recent experience. Being mindful occurs whenever you bring awareness to what you are directly experiencing via your senses or your mental state via your thoughts and emotions. Additionally, there is mounting evidence that when you train your brain to be mindful, you are altering the physical structure of your brain.

When practicing mindfulness, life exists only in the here and now. The moment we are experiencing is pure. Mindfulness is a "living" meditation practice that you can engage in throughout your precious life. There is no need to flee to a remote location to practice mindfulness, as it can be practiced anywhere and at any time, regardless of what is happening around you. Because mindfulness is an effective method for self- awareness, stress reduction, and living in the present moment, cultivating mindfulness is a powerful therapeutic practice.

The practice of mindfulness interrupts the mind's natural propensity for wandering and strengthens the ability to concentrate. Mindfulness entails concentrating your attention on a single object and monitoring the objects that capture your attention. When we improve our capacity for concentration, mindfulness becomes more straightforward, though this always requires some effort and time.

When we direct our attention to the body, we gradually develop an increased sensitivity to bodily sensations, even if only on our breath and posture. As our sensitivity to the field of bodily sensations increases, it becomes easier to maintain focus on the body and recognize when our attention is diverted to some other story. While absorbed in the field of awareness of bodily sensations, it is possible to relax the focus of attention and rest the mind gradually. When thought formations originate in awareness, it becomes possible to observe how attention shifts away from the field of sensations and then returns to it.

With practice, awareness can become so ingrained in the body that thought forms vanish before fully developing.

Not only does developing concentrative stabilization require effort, but it also requires a certain mentality. When our minds wander, becoming frustrated only adds to our agitation, and the effort we exert becomes a force of control. Concentration becomes a battleground as the chaotic mind struggles against the will's might.

Mindfulness Practice

Mindfulness enables us to establish a buffer zone between ourselves and our reactions, thereby dismantling our conditioned responses. **How to maintain a state of mindfulness throughout the day:**

1. **Allocate some time.** You do not need a meditation cushion or bench, or any other specialized equipment, to access your mindfulness abilities—but you will need some time and space.

2. **Acknowledge the present moment for what it is.** The purpose of mindfulness is not to quiet the mind or to achieve an eternal state of calm. The objective is straightforward: we want to pay attention to the present moment without passing judgment.

3. **Allow your judgments to pass you by.** When judgments arise during our practice, we can mentally note them and allow them to pass.

4. **Reintroduce yourself to observing the present moment as-is.** Frequently, our minds become absorbed in reflection. That is why mindfulness is defined as the practice of repeatedly returning to the present moment.

5. **Be patient with your mind's wanderings.** Make no judgments about whatever thoughts arise; instead, practice recognizing when your mind has wandered and gently bringing it back.

6. **Concentrate on your breathing.** When experiencing negative thoughts, take a seat, take a deep breath, and close your eyes. Concentrate

solely on your breath as you inhale and exhale. Even a minute spent sitting and breathing deeply can be beneficial.

It's frequently stated that it is extremely simple, but this is not always the case. The task is to continue doing it. The results will accumulate. It's simply right here, right now: fully immersing yourself in the present moment and experiencing life to the fullest.

It is truly that straightforward. It is easy to over-analyze, intellectualize, or complicate the concept of mindfulness. Naturally, our mind will make every effort to divert our attention but try not to let it. Recognize the presence of your analytical mind, greet it, and then dismiss it calmly. All that is required to be mindful is to be.

The Benefits of Mindfulness

· Mindfulness improves wellbeing.

Enhancing your capacity for mindfulness facilitates the development of numerous attitudes that contribute to a satisfying life. Being mindful enables you to savor the pleasures of life as they occur, to engage fully in activities, and to develop a greater capacity for dealing with adverse events. Many people who practice mindfulness discover that by focusing on the present moment, they are not worried about the future or regret the past, are less preoccupied with concerns about success and self-esteem, and are more capable of forming deep connections with others.

· Mindfulness improves physical health.

If increased wellbeing is insufficient motivation, scientists have discovered that mindfulness techniques benefit physical health in various ways. Mindfulness helps in the relief of stress, the treatment of heart disease, the reduction of blood pressure, the reduction of chronic pain, the improvement of sleep, and the alleviation of gastrointestinal problems. The list goes on.

• *Mindfulness improves mental health.*

Psychotherapists have increasingly used mindfulness meditation to treat various issues, including depression, substance abuse, eating disorders, couples' conflict, anxiety disorders, and obsessive-compulsive disorder.

Appreciation is the key. If it's a sunny day, appreciate its beauty and the vitamin D it gives you. If it's a rainy day, appreciate the water for drinking and helping the plants grow to bring us oxygen. If things start to go wrong just move on or change the subject. If you bang your elbow just laugh. Even though obviously it's not funny. Once you pick up the momentum with the good things in life, you'll notice more and more good.

If you wake up and get grumpy because it's raining and then bang your elbow and then get angry, then the negative momentum will draw you in and you'll have someone tooting at you. You could get stuck in more traffic than usual. Someone at the supermarket is rude to you. However you are feeling you draw that energy into your life.

If you're finding positive aspects in your life, then you're going to keep getting more of that. You may run into a grumpy person, but by flying high you just cruise past them. If you are stressed or grumpy like them, then you're going to run straight into their grump. It's like a magnet drawing you both together. So you're both saying "see," everyone is rude and grumpy. The Universe gives you total freedom. It's your choice to be grumpy. The Universe says if you want to be grumpy then here you go, I'll bring you more grumpy people so you can all hang out together.

It's completely up to you. I understand some days you really just don't care. That's fine. Just wake up the next day and try a little bit more to feel good. If you're having a bad day, just don't worry about it. You always have the next day and the next day and the next day to try again.

I try to focus on positive aspects of my life, the basic things which we are very lucky to have: I enjoy having food for my breakfast. I love my blankets and bed. I love having a car to drive in that has a heater and air conditioning. It's the little things throughout your day that start to make up the good feeling flow. I love my morning coffee. I love having water in my shower. Such simple things but if you can play the "appreciation game" then life gets better and better.

How can people in some extremely poor areas in different countries be so happy and healthy? Are they appreciating life and enjoying the little that they have? They are laughing and smiling and are totally grateful.

I know it's hard when you are comparing yourself to what's right in front of you. Just try and reach for the thought that feels better. Stop worrying about what others are doing.

Mind your own business.

Mind your own vibration.

If you've focused on behaviors you aren't happy with then just withdraw the negative attention. Wellbeing is the order of the Universe. If you're happy and feeling good, everyone you know will benefit from the association with you.

"They are like fresh air. That person feels good to be around. I want to suck up their pure positive energy." - Abraham Hicks

If you focus on yourself and ensure you're number one, then everyone around you will benefit. You will just have a feeling like you're invincible. I'm not saying every day is perfect because we have days when we are completely over it and can't be bothered but I find the more you meditate and connect to yourself and the energy source the easier it gets to snap out of your funk.

Stuff still happens around you because you can't control everyone else. If anything that's a bit more stressful happens you realize that contrast is valuable. It helps you learn; it helps you discover. It helps you appreciate life. Even if people around me are unwell or suffering, I have compassion but now I try to send love and positive vibes and realize that it's going to be ok. They are on their journey. They are also growing and evolving.

In the end, nothing really matters. If we turn into pure positive energy when we release our body, then those people who we thought were suffering have had amazing contrast so the buzz would be so incredible. Imagine going from pain and suffering then all of a sudden you release it all and you are pure positive energy. Total ecstasy. I mean, I don't think any of us could really describe it.

You release everything negative, you're floating, you're flowing, you have an amazing collection of all you have ever dreamt of manifested before your eyes. A lot of people that have had near-death experiences have not been happy being back because the feeling they had was so out of this world. The feeling of being in alignment. Total bliss. The white lights are tunnels that surround us, but we can't see them with our physical eyes. They take us to other realms. People often talk of white lights in operations or near-death experiences. There's such a sense of peace and calm. But we really need to appreciate this world with its resistance, with its contrast, with its pain. It makes us so much stronger in the end. It brings a lot of expansion and clarity.

I've heard people say you actually choose to come here to this beautiful planet, and you choose to come to poorer countries. To places with drought and no food. It seems completely crazy that you would choose to do this, but I find a lot of comfort in it—the thought of people learning and expanding their talents and consciousness, learning from the massive contrast.

A lot of people live in terrible places, but they have brain and heart coherence. They have love and joy in their hearts, and some can be happier than millionaires.

Total appreciation of everything and everyone is amazing, but it takes a while to get into the habit of it. I learned to just let go completely of everything. Well, maybe 80 percent control. I'm working on it every day. I just look at the basic things in life and fully take it in as much as I can. I have mostly stopped trying to control what anyone else is doing. Children, adults, animals all have their own guidance and their own journey to live. We feel we have to control them all so that we can be happy, or we feel we are helping them in some way.

As soon as I really learned to let go it was the biggest relief I have ever felt. There was a deep knowing that everything was ok. A wave of relaxation came over me. If you looked at me now, you might say that's insensitive or lazy. I have found by not overcompensating and trying to help everyone the people around me are happier and are learning through their own experiences. Words don't teach as much as actually having experienced something.

Instead of trying to help people do things I try and role model instead. I focus on the things that are going well which is so much easier than focusing on what's going wrong.

What are you appreciating in your life?

-
-
-

Sometimes you wonder why you do things when your brain says no but your heart says yes. I'm discovering how magical the heart really is and how it's not just here to pump blood around the body delivering oxygen and nutrients. It has an innate wisdom which guides us and supports us. Like the gut has intelligence the heart also has intelligence. It stores memory and can guide you. It's amazing how we actually have three "brains."

CHAPTER 9

THE QUANTUM WORLD

*"We are what we think. All that we are arises with our thoughts.
With our thoughts, we make the world."*

- BUDDHA

There is a field that connects everything. Like a matrix. It's a field of intelligent energy. There has been talk about the Divine matrix. The container for the entire Universe. It's a bridge between our inner and outer worlds. Consciousness controls the physical world not the other way around.

Quantum Wellness

Every thought is still energy flowing throughout the Universe. You are able to tap into these thoughts accidentally or on purpose. That's why sometimes you have the most random thought pop into your mind or you receive the most amazing thoughts.

I have found researching quantum physics & epigenetics has been such a life changer. Who would have thought someone that really didn't care about school would be up late at night studying the quantum world. I think I love it because it explains so much about the Universe in a way where it all starts to make sense. Before so much stuff about the Universe was so "woo woo" or "mystical." You were called crazy, got locked up or worse. Our minds, knowledge and understanding of the Universe are expanding and evolving. We can no longer live in the old belief systems, paradigms of the past. We are so much more than we think we are. We are so much more powerful, creative, and knowledgeable.

You know how sometimes you can feel the negative energy when you're in a room with two people who are mad at each other, even if they aren't obviously angry? They might not have said anything, and they could be smiling but you still know something just went down.

More and more scientists are beginning to realize that we aren't just physical. We have electromagnetic properties, which are also called our electric biofield, chi (q), aura, etc.

Your aura protects you, supports your immune system, and projects energy. They say it is what is damaged when you're exposed to too many EMFs (electromagnetic frequencies). I wouldn't over think that, but I do believe it's important to keep your mind and energy body healthy, then your physical body is feeling good as well.

Apparently, our hearts are five thousand times magnetically stronger than our brains. The heart is the most powerful source of electromagnetic energy in the human body. You might notice when you're meditating your heart feels like it's expanding. I find my heart expands at other times as well. I might be at the beach, and I can feel the breeze. I might be proud of a loved one, and it expands. It feels like your chest is tightening. When you get used to it this experience can feel amazing. You are aligned with your higher self.

"What is quantum physics? Put simply, it's the physics that explains how everything works: the best description we have of the nature of the particles that make up matter and the forces with which they interact." - newscientist. com

All matter is made of particles/waves that are called atoms. Which are in turn made of protons, neutrons and electrons. Inside is energy. Matter takes on different forms depending on how it's arranged. I've seen experiments being done by leading scientists. They shot particles in different directions. They were fourteen miles apart. Whatever they would do to one particle the other had the same experience at the same time. It seemed like they were still physically connected. Once matter is physically connected, it's always linked energetically even if it's miles apart.

We are all connected through quantum entanglement. That's how some people know something has happened to a loved one and they can be across the other side of the world. Distance doesn't matter because we are energetically connected.

What you believe you perceive and what you perceive you experience. You don't just need to accept what's happening. If you are ill or have an injury, you don't just have to accept that it's going to be that way.

We can heal ourselves and we can make ourselves ill.

After studying a bit of quantum physics and epigenetics it leads me to believe more and more that stress is causing so many illnesses and injuries. Your body has its own functional healing system but if you are blocking it by being angry, worried, frustrated and fearful you only disallow the amazing flow of natural healing.

You cannot control the world, but you can control how you react to it. At the core of everyone's being is love, wellness, joy and happiness. All anyone really wants is to be happy. Everyone has different opinions about what is going to be best for themselves or the collective. You can't get in other people's heads and change their belief systems and thoughts. You can control your own thoughts.

Sometimes when you are caught up in drama, the momentum has built up and it can take longer to get off that runaway train, but you can do it day by day. Slowly recognizing your thoughts. Realizing you can't change the news, but the news can change you. It is far better for the collective as a whole to send love rather than hate. To be understanding rather than frustrated. To send kindness rather than judgement. Remember not to judge yourself if you're not having a good day. The contrast of what you don't want sends amazing dreams and desires into the Universe. What you're putting out into the Universe comes back.

Energy never ends. It just transforms. Energy is information.

The mind heals the body. The mind can disrupt and become disharmonious with the body to make it ill. Genes aren't just the fixed state you are born with.

We are here for deliberate conscious expansion. Attention to something causes it to amplify.

I love looking deeper into the quantum world and discovering some amazing things. It used to be called "miracles," people healing, people moving objects. It's all becoming reality now. Dr Joe Dispenza explains the "placebo effect" and how we can tell our mind and bodies we are healing. He explains it better than me but pretty much he has investigated when pharmaceutical companies create a new drug they add a sugar pill to the trial. They noticed a number of people would heal themselves and all they had was a pill with nothing but starch or sugar. Placebo pills are made to look exactly like a real drug. The scientific research is proving we can actually heal our own bodies. The power of the mind.

The best results are through meditation. It has been helping so many people heal themselves. They let go of the stuck resistance and emotions.

We are just cruising around in our realities, having no idea that we are a powerful consciousness that is connected to the Universe. We can tap into anything anywhere. Our consciousness is like Google, a search engine able to download anything we want. We are just so distracted with what's right in front of us that we have lost the bigger picture. Years of beliefs have conditioned the world to think they are just a human being struggling to get through life. Some believe we die then hopefully go to somewhere amazing. Or if we are "bad" we might go to "hell".

Some grew up not really believing there's anything at all out there and that once we die that's it. You're done.

You cannot tell me anymore that we have the perfect amount of oxygen for human beings just accidentally. That we are in the exact right spot between the sun and the moon. That cells by themselves turned into these magnificent living breathing beings. I've heard scientists say that the odds of our earth turning into what it is today is like a tornado coming through and assembling a Boeing 747 jet plane.

If you look online and search Wikipedia you can read about The **junkyard tornado**, also known as **Hoyle's Fallacy.** It's said it "is an argument used to deride the probability of abiogenesis as comparable to "the chance that a tornado sweeping through a junkyard might assemble a Boeing 747." It was used originally by Fred Hoyle, in which he applied statistical analysis to the origin of life, but similar observations predate Hoyle and have been found all the way back to Darwin's time," Quote from en.m.wikipedia.org

Abiogenesis meaning the original evolution of life or living organisms.

"Your belief carries more power than your reality." - Bruce Lipton

We are more than what we think we are. Our bodies can heal. Stress shuts off growth & maintenance, so it affects the body, including the gut. Stress can shut off the immune system or slow it down.

I attended an interesting lecture with stem cell biologist, Bruce Lipton. Who said "We are very powerful in controlling our biology."

We are not being chased by saber-toothed tigers but our subconscious body acts like it. This puts our immune system at risk. You can see why so many people get sick. Every day I try to do a little bit more to become aware of what I'm putting into my body and on my body. Stress, pharmaceuticals, processed foods, sprays on fruits and veggies, chemicals in skin care products. Our skin is one big organ. If you wouldn't drink it, why would you put it on your skin? I still don't want to overthink anything, though. The more you think it's harmful the more you can create harm.

Just be calm about it and let your intuition guide you. I promise you I'm far from perfect on what I've done to my body and my mind. Life is about living and having fun. In the end we are energy so we should be able to transform anything we do or eat into a positive form.

So many of us are living in survival mode. When we are in that state, we narrow our focus. We become materialistic. The brain starts to subdivide and sends us to an incoherent state.

A huge number of scientists, life coaches and doctors are talking about the mind and how most of the time we are not even conscious. We are actually on autopilot listening to our thoughts and feelings that half the time aren't even real. Belief systems and past experiences have left us in an auto loop. Experts believe we have around fifty to eighty thousand thoughts a day. So much stress and worry from random, negative thoughts or just thoughts that don't serve you. Thoughts that aren't even ours.

We could actually spend our days more conscious and aware. We could spend our days enjoying every moment instead of waiting for something amazing in the future. Why do we spend our time saying, "As soon as I've made enough money to buy that then I'll be happy"? "As soon as I go on that trip I'll be having fun." Why can't we be happy and have fun all of the time? Do we need to get to a final destination to be happy?

Life is such a gift. We get to experience so many amazing things.

"Your personality creates your personal reality" – Dr. Joe Dispenza.

So, if you're creating chaos in your mind then you can create chaos in your outer world. If you're saying you have no money, then you will feel like you don't have money. If you say you feel sick all the time, then you will feel sick. Put out what you would like to attract. It's like two magnets coming together.

When I first was told, "We are like a computer," I thought that was the most random thing I'd heard but then as I continued to study quantum physics I realized we are more like a computer than we think. We download software (belief system/ blocks). We have a ram. We collect so many unwanted thoughts that our memory gets full. Our brain is an operating system. All of our thoughts are cluttering up our brains and we struggle to remember everything. That's where meditation comes in handy because you can clear out all the unwanted and reset your brain and your focus and connection again.

With our busy lifestyles and ever-growing wants and needs, we put ourselves under more stress. Even driving to work in the traffic can be stressful and we haven't even started our day yet.

We are more often than not in a fight, flight, or freeze "survival" mode where our instincts tell us we are in danger. Through busy lifestyles, stress, and commitments. Just the thought of getting somewhere on time can put you into survival mode.

The news, social media, keeping up with friends, family commitments—it can all be overwhelming some days. But does it really need to be that stressful? Are we overreacting more than we need to?

Life is such a beautiful journey. There are the most amazing things out there happening every second of every day. A lot of us are starting to lose connection with the magical world of nature and with ourselves.

It's time to unite. Send peace and love to everyone out there. If your heart is full of love and forgiveness, you can have a much more beautiful, enjoyable life. We get to live this human existence. It is actually such a gift to experience the good and the bad. We are lucky to be alive and have these amazing sensory experiences.

We can also go deeper into our minds and unlock the magic from within. Our minds are so much more capable than we ever imagined. Our mind/ body/soul are so connected. If you are busy in "fight, flight or freeze" mode you will start to lose the connections. You can become unwell, and life is not as enjoyable.

You can "rewire" your brain and create an amazing outer environment full of love and abundance. It can take time so keep persevering. But just remember, when you notice your unwanted thoughts, then that's a "victory."

Clear the unwanted thoughts. I started by trying to send my thoughts away in bubbles. Then I started facing some of them that I knew were easier to control. I definitely didn't agree with a lot of my thoughts. I've replaced so many of them with positive affirmations:

I am happy, I am healthy, I am abundance, I am beautiful, I am worthy. The thoughts that I can't get rid of I just send them away with the butterflies or you can bury them or put them in an inactive box. It's up to you how you want to visualize it. Often I'll turn the unwanted thoughts into flowers or energy for trees, I don't want my random thoughts going to someone else that doesn't need them.

I watched *Rewired* with Dr Joe Dispenza and read his book *Becoming Supernatural*. He teaches you how to get past the mind. Past the unwanted thoughts. Un-memorize those survival emotions that naturally lower the frequency of the mind and the body. Replace them with a feeling of wholeness, love, and balance, feeling a sense of love for life.

The environment signals the genes. What you are thinking you are creating. If you're thinking you're ill, you can continue to think that. If you are visualizing being healed your brain starts to believe you are. What you think about, you bring about.

Neurons (also called brain cells or nerve cells) are the fundamental units of the brain and nervous system, the cells responsible for receiving sensory input from the external world, for sending motor commands to our muscles, and for transforming and relaying the electrical signals at every step in between.

There are photos on scientific websites showing a picture of a brain which shows neurons and then there are other pictures taken of galaxies. They look very similar. These connections have been found through gravitational photography. In the naked darkness of space light is bending itself. They are ionic plasma channels, organized sharing between galaxies. So pretty much what it's saying is that the inside of our brain looks like the Universe. The galaxies. The question was asked: Is it a super mind that we are a part of? Can we access this super mind? Or are we modelled off the galaxies? We have so much potential. We are all made of stardust. Literally.

We can also keep rewiring our brains. If they are injured or something happens, they can actually regenerate. It also means we can continue to learn and expand as we get older.

"neuroplasticity

/ˌnjʊərəʊplaˈstɪsɪti/

noun

1. The ability of the brain to form and reorganize synaptic connections, especially in response to learning or experience or following injury. "Neuroplasticity offers real hope to everyone from stroke victims to dyslexics." Information is from - Oxford.com

If you have something happen in your life, then the continuous explanation of what you have lived doesn't let you move on.

Don't forget to have fun and enjoy life. Think of everything as that you *get* to experience it, not that you *have* to. Even the bad. We still get to experience it. Then we continue to evolve and learn.

The Universe is expansive. There are billions of planets and stars in our galaxy alone. Earth is such a magical place. It's in the perfect spot between the sun and the moon. They call it The Goldilocks spot.

We are lucky here on Earth because we have time and space. A lot of scientists think other dimensions don't have time and space. I heard one scientist say it's the difference between an old tape and music streaming. With the tape you're slowly moving forward. If there's no time and space then you can skip to the next song like you would on your playlist. You jump anywhere at any time because there is no time. But I often hear that this is where it's at. This world we live in is cutting edge and full of expansion and excitement. Because we have what we call "time" it makes us create and expand a lot faster than a place that has no time. We are moving forward at a faster pace. The Universe wants to see what it can become. It wants to keep evolving, so it doesn't look back as much as we do. I feel sometimes it's like an excited child saying, "What's next?"

"We are actually invisible. We are only seen because of Photons in lights and from the sun" - Bruce H. Lipton, PHD.

We are made up of energy which is vibration and frequency. We are atoms and so if you look inside with the high-tech equipment science has these days we can prove it.

Are You Vibrationally Balanced?

Your thoughts & feelings help you understand what vibration or frequency you are on. It's the little things that make up your vibrational balance. Try to reach for the thoughts and words that feel good. Find words that make you feel more at ease. Every day you can practice finding better-feeling ways to express yourself. You are the only one that can bring yourself peace. You can't ask the outside world to provide it. Move on from old habits and old problems and start focusing on and appreciating all that you have.

To feel good, appreciation is the key. Have you actually truly looked at our world? The beautiful wonders of it. Remember when you were a kid and so excited about the sand or a flower or a butterfly. We get so overwhelmed and distracted by all of the other things around us—Work, media, life—that we forget how absolutely incredible our world is.

I am conscious and aware, and I am here.

Consciousness is paying attention and being aware. Do you observe your thoughts? Don't let that thought run you like a computer program. Is it really you?

Meditation means to become familiar with. So meditation can allow you to find your true essence. Your true authentic self. Live in creation rather than live in survival.

Are you present with yourself? Are you paying attention?

We are designed to survive but in today's world, we have been taking it too literally. Just everyday traffic is stressing us out. If we are not at ease, we can get a disease. Dis-ease equals disease.

I'm changing my perception. I want to become a master of my mind.

There are so many third world countries that can't afford specialists or pharmaceuticals, so they continue to use their innate wisdom from ancient times. In the western world, we have so many pills that are here to fix us, but they end up causing other ailments.

It's not the pharmaceutical companies fault. We asked for more ways to fix ourselves. They developed all of these drugs because that's what we were asking for. Quick easy fixes. A lot of it does help but a huge amount of times you end up with other things going wrong so it's best to get advice from all avenues. While you're healing with your doctor, for example, you can focus on things that make you feel good. Healing meditations. Visualize being healed and use mindfulness skills. Hopefully you will get to the root cause of the problem and release it. You don't need to know what the actual problem or block is. You just need to intend on releasing it.

Quantum Physics

Quantum physics is undoubtedly one of the biggest intellectual achievements in human civilization's history, but it appears to some people to be too remote and abstract to matter.

Without an understanding of history, quantum physics will make no sense. This history begins with Max Planck, continues with Albert Einstein and Niels Bohr, and culminates with scientists such as Schrödinger and Heisenberg in the current theory. This history helps us in understanding why scientists believe the Universe is fundamentally strange. Max Planck, a German theoretical physicist, accidentally founded the field of quantum mechanics (quantum physics) in 1900 while attempting to explain why the results of his experiment did not conform to the laws of classical physics. He discovered that energy is emitted in small packets (quanta) and appears to be emitted in wavelengths.

Since then, Einstein and other physicists have used his research to advance quantum physics, the branch of science concerned with the behavior of matter and energy on the atomic (and subatomic) scales. To comprehend quantum physics, we have to abandon all sense of logic. Why? Unlike classical physics, quantum physics disregards the logic that governs our everyday lives. Quantum particles obey a different set of laws, which we do not fully understand at the moment.

Today's Universe is not the same as yesterday's. Each moment brings a series of subtle but significant changes, many of which are indistinguishable on measurable, human timescales. The expansion of the Universe means that the distances between the largest cosmic structures are increasing over time. The Universe was slightly smaller a second ago; it will be slightly larger a second from now. We are helping to expand the Universe by everything we are doing.

By applying physical laws to the Universe we can determine both our origin and destination. We can extrapolate our history back to the big bang and even further back to a period of cosmic inflation..

CHAPTER 10

CREATING OUR WORLD

*"The basis of your life is freedom: the purpose of your life is joy.
You are a creator; you create with your every thought. As you are
choosing your thought, your emotions are guiding you."*

- ABRAHAMHICKS.COM

The Law of Vibration

Vibrating is a term that refers to oscillation, quivering, and rapid backward and forward movement. Everything vibrates on a subatomic level. At this level, matter and energy perform this function. Right now, the chair in which you are seated is vibrating violently. You cannot feel or see it because the molecules, atoms, and subatomic particles that comprise your chair are compact and minuscule. Matter vibrates at such a high rate of speed that we can't detect it unless we use an extremely powerful microscope. It is entirely true, due to the fact that everything is made up of vibrational energy. Even consciousness is made up of extremely fast-vibrating energy. This means our thoughts do have some weight. This is the vibrational law. Everything has a vibrational signature that can be quantified.

Each atom and molecule of energy in the universe vibrates. Everything vibrates at the moment, from the sun's rays to the atoms in your body. The law of vibration investigates this phenomenon. All known forms of energy are vibrational. Heat can be thought of as a unit of vibration. The more difficult it is for atoms to move within something, the higher the temperature. Electromagnetic energy exemplifies the wide variations in frequency. Vibratory energy is extremely powerful. I had no idea about the law of vibration and freaked out when I realized that everything was vibration. My friend who is amazingly knowledgeable started to explain it to me and I thought at first it sounded absolutely ridiculous. She told me that everything was energy and everything in the Universe vibrated. Perhaps oxygen makes sense, but what about my hand, body, a car, or a huge building? This seemed so weird and crazy. It felt like I was watching a sci-fi movie.

When I finally realized that the entire Universe is made up of moving atoms, I was taken back by the implications. This meant that things could be altered; if we follow the logic, diseases were also just frequencies vibrating within the law of vibration.

Your vibration is the level of emotional energy and connection to the Universe that exists within your body and consciousness. It is your current inner state, your frequency sensation, and having a high frequency enables you to manifest your desires and succeed. Prioritizing high frequency may be the most efficient way to accomplish all of your other goals and dreams.

The law of vibration is critical to comprehending Universal consciousness. If everything is vibrational and communication between things is instantaneous, we are connected to something much larger than we ever imagined.

Science has recently discovered that metaphysical laws have evolved into their laws and theories. Through quantum physics research, science confirms what metaphysics has known for thousands of years—that everything and everyone is connected. Each of us is a unique being, but we are also a component of the Universal consciousness that comprises the whole. As is the case with a drop of saltwater from a vast ocean larger than our solar system, that drop of water remains a part of the ocean, as is the case with each of us.

We can communicate with the Universal consciousness through our vibrational signatures because we are a part of it. This law of vibration is also a component of a larger picture. This is why the law of attraction works in our favor. The key to applying the law of vibration is to increase your vibrational frequency to a positive value, a good vibration. The Universal consciousness will reciprocate the higher vibration with which you begin to resonate. Similarity attracts similarity. Alternatively, light attracts light. The Super Consciousness responds to the thoughts, feelings, and emotions you send out and manifests them into your life.

The larger picture is the law of attraction. It's an excellent communicator. We communicate our consciousness to the Universal consciousness through our vibrational patterned signatures, and the Universal consciousness responds by sending us our reality. Whether for good or ill, we receive what we give. The law does not make judgments about what is right or wrong; we do. This law returns to us following the vibrational frequency that we emit. We have total freedom. We can choose to have bad things happen to us. The Universe lets us have whatever we want. The good and the bad. Be careful what you wish for.

As you maintain your focus on the present moment, you begin to sense the energy of your surroundings. To sensitize yourself to the energy that surrounds you, maintain a conscious awareness of the present moment. The majority of people sleepwalk through their lives, oblivious to details. And this is why they create unnecessary drama in their lives.

Consciousness and vibrational frequency are inextricably linked. If you are conscious, you can easily pick up on others' vibes. It becomes more straightforward than deciding who to interact with and who to avoid. Maintain an awareness of the present moment to perceive the vibrations of people and objects around you. Also I have to note again that if your present moment sucks, then it is hard to live in the now. That's where you can begin to work on lifting your vibration every day.

While this may sound unbelievable, numerous resources explain in great detail what science in quantum physics has discovered about reality's cause and effect. Nature is one of intent. None of this requires you to be a rocket scientist or a metaphysical guru to work. Understanding that the Universal consciousness can work for you, as well as a willingness to let go of outdated beliefs about yourself and your relationship with the Universe, is enough—discovering abundance, genuine happiness, and quality of life you never imagined.

Your vibration determines the nature of your reality. If you are dissatisfied with the results in your life, you must make a conscious decision to alter your vibrational frequency. You can get this by simply focusing on a positive thought. As your vibration increases, you will attract similar vibrations into your conscious awareness. As a result, you will attract the success, prosperity, and experiences you desire. Simply put, you will take control of your life.

Ways to use the law of vibration:

1. Appreciation
Expressing appreciation is the simplest way to boost your vibration. You can do this mentally, aloud, or by scribbling in a journal. Your vibrational energy increases when you express appreciation for what you have in your life. As a result, your thoughts, emotions, and actions become more positive, and wonderful things begin to manifest in your life.

2. Speak Positively
Do this whenever you are confronted with disempowering thoughts and emotions. In your mind, say five positive statements for every negative thought. This effectively eliminates negative thoughts and reprogrammed

the subconscious mind. Most importantly, develop a habit of positive self-talk. Your conscious mind can be used to imprint positive ideas on the subconscious. As you choose positivity consciously in your life, you develop a high vibrational being. By speaking strong, happy, and empowering words, you can alter your vibration.

3. Eat High-Vibe Food

Bring your mind back into focus as soon as it begins to stray from the present moment. The more you concentrate on the "now," the more aware you will become of your vibration. You can alter your vibration to your advantage. On the other hand, stale foods, and foods containing preservatives and artificial colors have low vibrations. I would take this with a grain of salt because I still believe if it makes you feel good then everything in moderation. As a result, develop a habit of mostly eating fresh and healthy foods to raise your vibration. You can easily discover how food affects your body's vibrational frequency. Food that makes you feel good from the inside out is considered high vibe food. (I still do 80/20 because life on Earth is all about smelling and tasting and living. I don't like to be strict. I find that boring and makes me want more.)

Buddha Bowl: *Have you tried recreating your own?* There are thousands of different fun recipes you can try for a different look. Buddha Bowls are a healthy, nutritious option. Check out Pinterest for yummy ideas.

4. Stop Gossiping

When you speak ill of someone, even in secret, you immediately begin emitting negative energy. We are all energy beings connected to the source of energy. Thus, even if you make a negative remark behind someone's back, energy flows to them and is felt. They, too, unconsciously return the negative vibe to you, and you are trapped in this circle indefinitely. Most importantly, if you want to maintain a positive vibe at all times, refrain from saying negative things about others. Take care with your words, as they affect the frequency of your energy. Gossiping and backstabbing never benefit anyone; they only serve to instill negativity in your mind and environment. Don't worry, we are not all perfect and sometimes we just need to get it all out. Personally, if someone annoyed me when I was first practicing this I would send love like I was killing them with kindness instead of being annoyed. It helps me and I get the good vibes coming back to me.

5. Smiling Frequently

Laughter has several beneficial effects. It can heal and boost your energy in an instant. You truly do not require an occasion to smile! You hear about people healing themselves by watching funny movies. Laughter is such a high vibration.

6. Align Your Vibration with Your Aspirations

If you desire something, align your vibration with that frequency. Bring similar energies into your life or expose yourself to them. Therefore, if you want to improve your health, begin by stocking your refrigerator with fresh fruits and vegetables. If you want to be a musician, purchase a guitar or, better yet, get a lesson.

7. Surround Yourself with Higher Vibrations

If you want to benefit from the law of vibration and become a successful person, begin networking with people who have a high vibration. Interact with people who are accomplishing similar things in life. Use others as inspiration rather than being jealous of what they have achieved. Raising your vibration is the quickest way to shift your vibration and alter the course of your life.

8. Utilize a Vision Board.

Images that reflect your ideal life can be found on Google or Pinterest. There are heaps of cool websites for ideas. What kind of home do you want to live in, what kind of car do you want to drive, what kind of lifestyle do you envision for yourself, and with who do you see yourself socializing with? Make a point of downloading all images that reflect your ideal life.

Now, here's the kicker! This has nothing to do with the life you are currently living or your current situation. No. Take a screenshot of each image that represents your ideal life. Print out these images, cut and arrange them and glue them together on a poster board. This is referred to as a vision board.

You can hang this vision board in an area that you will see frequently throughout the day. You can also just do one on your computer or iPad and print it out or just keep it for reference on your device. You can also make "Mind Movies" which is the same concept, but it's a digital video. You can add music for inspiration and motivation. The more you visualize your dream life, the more you begin to vibrate at a higher frequency. As a result, you begin to attract unexpected opportunities that lead you closer to the life of your dreams.

9. Spend Time in Nature

Spending time alone in nature is one of the simplest ways to raise your vibration and work with the law of vibration in your favor. The more time you spend in natural environments, the higher your vibrational frequency will be. Take a stroll along the beach or embark on a mountain trek. Alternatively, you can sit daily beneath a tree to absorb the natural high vibrations.

10. Practice Mindfulness

Our mind is constantly wandering. Concentrate on the present moment by practicing mindfulness. Meditation is said to increase one's concentration. Alternatively, you can continue observing your thoughts. Bring your mind back into focus as soon as it begins to stray from the present moment. The more you concentrate on the "now," the more aware you will become of your vibration. You can alter your vibration to your advantage.

Creating Your Own Reality

A couple of widely talked about phenomenon are "The Law of Attraction," and you "create your own reality." This to me is a bit like Google, Pinterest, Amazon, and all of the big search engines. The law of attraction brings you what it thinks you want. The Universe uses vibration and frequency to connect. So if you are putting out a vibration (feeling) of vulnerability, anger, frustration, and sadness then you will get a reflection of those things back to you.

If you want good things to come make sure you focus on what makes you feel good. Focus on what puts you at ease. If it doesn't come, it's because you have resistance to it. You might have belief systems that slow you down. You may not feel worthy. You may not believe in the abundance that you deserve. It's all there waiting for us. Notice your thoughts and feelings. All of the negativity can just cause disease so focus on the good. Create your own reality by drawing in the pure love of the Universe.

Your guidance system is always there. If you're seeing negativity it's because you've been focusing on it and the law of attraction is bringing it to you. Stop the momentum of negative thoughts. Calm your mind. Do whatever you can to make yourself feel good. Meditation, mindfulness, massage, walks. Try to manifest or visualize something for fun. I talked about how I tried manifesting butterflies at the beginning. You just ask to bring them into your life, and they come in weird and wonderful ways. It seems silly manifesting butterflies, but the Universe loves to play and it's such a simple easy request that doesn't have years of resistance on it. You're not overthinking the butterflies like you would if you were asking for money. You would expect to see a butterfly, but you wouldn't expect to see money.

What can you bring in with the law of attraction? We started with yellow cars so when we saw a yellow car we would give ourselves $1000 per car and $1000 for charity. Different sizes are of a different value. It sounds like a game of I spy, but you will see things in the most random unexpected places and ways. You're bringing money into your vibration for fun with that game as well.

Gratitude is such a huge word at the moment. It has the vibration of thankfulness for overcoming something. Overcoming something still has some resistance to it. Appreciation has less resistance, but the word gratitude is still one of the highest vibrational words. I use appreciation all of the time now. If I can appreciate every single thing good and bad, then I am more in alignment with who I truly am.

The feeling of empathy means you've lived it. You join a person in that vibration. This is what takes you to lower levels of feeling bad. Compassion is remaining in alignment with who you really are. You stay where you are in order to call someone's vibration higher. Having compassion for someone means you're not lowering your own good feeling.

Our Vibrational World

"There is a vibrational energetic environment that's there." - Abraham Hicks

It's the manifestation, the desires, the dreams but it is not yet the physical manifestation that we call matter (matter is denser energy). We have visualized what we want, and it's right there in front of us as a vibrational environment. It's right there but most of us can't see this vibrational world. We can just see the vibrational world that is physically manifested. Our visual perception and belief systems won't let us see it.

All these amazing things we have wished for, dreamt, and desired are right there in front of us.

We get frustrated if they haven't physically manifested and we think they will never happen or it's too hard. Those things we want are right there in front of us, dangling in front of us like a carrot in front of a horse. We just need to believe we can have them.

I often talk about the top athletes and coaches and how they visualize already getting the goal. Achieving the win. It's the power of positive thinking. The power of the mind. This stuff really works.

You have to remember it can do the opposite. They say, "Be careful what you wish for." If you are fed up with your job, with your body, with everything around you then you can end up putting negative attention on certain areas. The Universe will keep bringing you negativity. Not because the Universe is mean but because you have total freedom and if you want the negative experiences, then you are allowed them. If you want to feel miserable, you can have that. The law of attraction gives you what you want. You can have the bad things. It's up to you. It's all about freedom. We can't just be thinking that the law is going to just bring us all of the good stuff even if we are saying our life is hard and being negative about a lot of areas in our life.

You have the choice. If you want to focus on the bad, then focus on it and draw more of it into your life. It's your journey. If you want more good things, then you need to focus on good things. Focus on feeling better every day. Everything you attract can become more and more and more. Positively or negatively.

Let go of anything that doesn't support what you don't want.

Stop saying:

I don't feel good.

I don't have enough money.

I don't like my job.

I don't have a relationship.

My kids are frustrating.

My partner is annoying.

I'm suffering from something that happened ten years ago.

My body is falling apart.

I'm going to get sick because it's in my genes or DNA.

What do you expect to happen when you keep saying negative stuff to yourself? You have to stop focusing on what you don't want and start focusing on what you do want.

Don't compare yourself to anyone else. Focus on yourself. Find what's going to make your life easier. Don't swim against the current. Just flow downstream. There will be things that you don't really want to do but find the path that is slightly easier. What path is going to be easier and what path is going to be harder? Yes, you have the freedom to choose anything but sometimes what you are choosing is the opposite to most of the world. So is it easier just to find the path of least resistance? The path of most allowance?

Just a reminder, if you are focusing on things that are negative then that's what you're going to get. I'm meaning all of the darker arts. Going hunting for haunted houses. Ouija board (spirit board). You get what you expect with things like that. If you're in for a good scare and you like bringing negative energies in, if it makes you feel good, then I'm not saying don't do it. I'm just saying you get back what you're putting out there.

I'm a scaredy cat so I don't like watching any horrible movies or anything like that. The lower energies of the world just hang around that kind of stuff. That's why you see so many accidents when people are making those movies. It can affect mental health as well, allowing stress and anxiety to become bigger.

After we transition back to the pure positive energy of the Universe then all of that stuff is left on Earth so in the end it doesn't really matter. I just like to feel good, that's why I stay away from all of that. It's your decision; you can choose whatever you want. I know a lot of people love scary movies.

The Law of Attraction

"The mind is everything. What you think you become" – Buddha.

The law of attraction is a unifying principle that states that you will attract whatever you focus on into your life. Whatever you direct your energy and attention toward, that is what you will receive.

When you concentrate on the abundance of good things in your life, you will naturally attract more of the same. However, suppose you focus exclusively on negative thoughts and what you lack in life. In that case, you will eventually attract negativity into your life, and what you truly desire will continue to elude you.

Everyone, whether conscious of it or not, utilizes the law of attraction. If the mindset is that something is lacking in life, that is what is focused on, and that "lack" is still being attracted into that person's life. To reverse this trend, deliberate thought is required. That individual only needs to shift their focus to thinking as if the "lack" has already been filled. As if it were already theirs. The truth is that there are certain positive principles that you can begin applying immediately that will dramatically improve your life in a short time.

The Law of Attraction States:

Thoughts are things, and you attract into your life whatever you think about. This is an electromagnetic Universe, and we are electromagnetic beings. Your thoughts are energy, and whatever you direct your attention and energy toward will grow. Whether you truly desire illness, poverty, bankruptcy, unhappiness, or loneliness, you will obtain them if you think about it enough.

This law is as precise as "gravitational law." When the law of gravity kills the person who walks off the top of the mountain, it is not unkind or vindictive; it is simply the "law of gravity." We don't criticize the law of gravity but rather respect it. The law of attraction remains constant. Respect it and work with it; work against it, and you will encounter difficulties.

As a result, because it can only give you what you focus on, if you think about being broke, poor, sick, unlucky, or worn out, that is precisely what you will become. This law applies to your life and the lives of every other person on the planet. As with all Universal laws, it is unbiased and impersonal, which means that it operates regardless of whether you are discussing what you want or don't want.

How to Use the Law of Attraction

Are you interested in learning how to manifest your ideal life through the law of attraction? If you want to learn how to apply the law of attraction properly, you must first grasp a critical aspect of its operation. You attract what you think about, whether something you want or something you don't want. The law of attraction is a nonpartisan power, which implies it is unconcerned with positive or negative feelings or considerations. It simply accepts what you are offering. For instance, if you think, "I hope this traffic does not cause me to get into a car accident," you are initiating the process of causing a car accident. If, on the other hand, you're thinking, "I'm sure I'll make it home safely," you're ensuring just that—a safe ride home. It would be best to begin thinking deliberately to understand using the law of attraction to create your ideal life.

Raise your vibration: To understand how to effectively apply the law of attraction, you must first understand vibration. To achieve our desires, we must first be in vibrational harmony with them. When we feel good, optimistic, happy, or joyful, we are in vibrational harmony with our desires. When we are depressed, negative, anxious, or stressed, for example, we are out of balance. Using the law of attraction effectively requires achieving and maintaining happiness, which facilitates the flow of your desires.

Your thoughts shape your reality: To alter the course of your life, you must first alter your thoughts. When you develop an "appreciation behavior" and teach yourself to look on the bright side of life, you will notice that your life becomes more positive as a result!

Dream big: If you want the Universe to work miracles for you, you must dream big! Bear in mind that the Universe is constantly responding to the energy you send out.

Use positive affirmations: Using positive affirmations is the most effective way to keep your thoughts, actions, and energy focused on your highest goals. When you affirm that your goals have already been accomplished, you activate your subconscious mind to assist you in manifesting your vision!

Define your objectives: A well-defined vision results in well-defined outcomes. That is why it is critical to be specific about what you want— and to confirm that what you believe you want is truly what you want. Ambiguous desires produce ambiguous outcomes.

Create a vision board: Vision boards are an effective tool for clarifying your life vision and keeping your goals front of mind so they can be attracted effortlessly into your life.

Define a specific objective: Establish a goal that is specific, quantifiable, attainable, realistic and time-bound. Utilizing the law of attraction is a strategy for achieving your goals. Therefore, you must first establish a clear vision of what you desire. You don't have to know specifics. Just intend to be open and allowing to receive. When your intentions are clear, applying the law of attraction to yourself becomes effortless and enjoyable.

Loved Ones That Pass.

I've heard it's hard to connect with loved ones if you are trying to find them where they were. It's difficult to connect to them as now they are pure positive energy, so they aren't always exactly how you remember them. They have let go of all the resistance that is attached to a physical body. You can't find them when you feel like they have gone. You can't find them with your sadness. You can find them guiding and supporting you. If they were a stressed person, you won't find them stressed. If they were a worried person, you won't find them worried. If they had opinions in the past, now they will be supportive and understanding because they are a part of the bigger picture. They are pure love and light, so they are still themselves, but they have left any negativity that they had in their physical bodies behind. Let go of anything that makes you feel sad or makes you grieve. It's holding you in that same space. That's not where they are. They are so happy and healthy and they have let go of any negativity. You can find them when you're feeling good. Maybe walking along the beach and getting out in nature. You will find them in your excitement about something and remembering the good times and fun. You can't find them in their absence. Try and feel good then you can find them in your heart more easily. Focus on the present then you will sense them. If you're feeling up to it, you can put any items you have in a box, and this will help to inactivate your sadness or grief. Just know that they are fine and they are totally aware and supportive of what you do. They are in a good space.

If you can't feel good, then don't try. Just relax. Meditate, do some exercise. Reach for a thought that might feel slightly better. Have a rest. Shift your awareness to feel good. Stop trying to please everyone. Take care of yourself. You will get depleted if you focus on everyone else in your life and the world.

Don't think that people can't do things for themselves. Other people need to learn from their own experiences. You can't make everyone else's lives perfect. They need to go through what they do in order to learn and grow. If you are doing everything for everyone else, you're saying they can't do things for themselves.

You can't fix others. You can guide, support, and have compassion but don't bring yourself down to a lower level to feel their frustration, worry or sadness. You're only telling them that they can't fend for themselves.

Put your emphasis on how you feel. Don't try and fix everyone else. You must get yourself in a better feeling place. You can't help them if you're not in a good feeling space.

No one can heal you. It's up to you to heal yourself. Others can hold you in the space to help you heal but in the end, it's up to you to allow yourself to heal.

There are a lot of people out there, doctors, professional health care workers, healers. There are a huge number of amazing options to help you on your healing journey but in the end, if you don't want to heal or are focusing on your limitations then it's very hard for someone to help you. They may heal you for a while but sometimes you can end up still telling your old story and you are back at square one feeling unwell or upset again.

I am no expert at all. I have days where I change the subject in order to feel better. It does make sense to me though that we can try a little bit every day to focus on our wellness rather than our illness.

You get what you think about. Anytime you are feeling angry or hateful you aren't in alignment with who you really are. Your being is love and happiness. Good feels good because it is good. Don't focus on people that aren't putting out positive information.

Everyone is trying to work out their lives in the best way that they can. Anger will not lead you to what you want.

Don't regret anything. You can't fix what's already been. Live in the now. Try and think thoughts that feel better. It takes time at the beginning to look at your thoughts and tweak them to better feeling ones.

Appreciate your breathing. Appreciate the oxygen. Appreciate the little things.

Take the path of least resistance. The path of most allowance. You can't make everyone want the same things as you. You can't make everyone believe the same things as you.

If people are on a lower feeling emotion, it's very hard for you to bring them up to better feeling emotions. You need to focus on your own emotions rather than trying to fix everyone else.

Sometimes they will just find you frustrating if they are on a lower feeling emotion. They might be feeling worried or angry and your positivity only drives them crazy and makes them feel angrier.

"Before you say something think, is it true? is it helpful? "If it's not helpful then let it go" - Deepak Chopra.

The Emotional Guidance Scale

Abraham Hicks has an "Emotional Guidance Scale." It's such an amazing tool to find out where you're at.

The top starts with appreciation, love, joy, and freedom. You go further down the scale and at the bottom is fear, grief, powerlessness, despair.

Our feelings are our guidance system. It's hard to move straight up from being fearful, depressed, anxious to feeling amazing and happy. Your vibration is where it is, and it won't allow you to just skip way up to the top. You probably have got a lot of resistance, blocks and belief systems holding you back. You have momentum keeping your feelings active.

It's ok, it's not your fault. Not every day is perfect, and you feel amazing. You definitely learn a lot from the contrast, but I promise you it is possible when you do reach the higher end of the emotional scale to feel good more and more. You also have to realize that you could be feeling different emotions. It's not always just one emotion all day. You can have multiple emotions about different subjects.

Once you practice that higher vibration you really notice when you're not in it and you crave getting back on it. It doesn't seem worth going back to feeling bad. You wonder why you wasted all your time not enjoying life as much as you could have. Who would have thought that being happy makes you happy? It's seriously as easy as that. Once you get there, you'll look back and laugh at how simple it is to be happy.

Just keep trying every day. You can climb your way up and up by starting fresh every morning. If you have a bad day, don't worry about it because you would have learned, grown, and created expansion from the contrast. Just live in the now and stop reliving that "bad" day. It doesn't get you anywhere by over-analyzing it.

When you move up the emotional scale, it can actually seem like sometimes you're going backwards. So some people move from depression to anger. You may think it is terrible that someone is angry, but it's actually a higher vibration than being depressed and not wanting to do anything. The anger has more emotion. I'm not saying it's where you want to be, I'm just saying don't judge yourself or others for feeling angry. If they can focus their anger and release it and find better feeling thoughts, then they can move up the scale.

Getting rid of anger, frustration and sadness can actually be really fun. You can find things to help release it. There are so many amazing options out there. Don't hold on to your anger, sadness, frustrations, and worries. You will only create blocks and that build-up can give you pain and illnesses over time. Release it in a constructive way.

People can tell you that it's not good to be angry, but they don't realize that you've actually moved up the emotional scale. Having feelings is an improvement from being completely depressed lying on the couch. You're up and going again. I definitely wouldn't want anyone to get stuck in a pattern of feeling angry but it's a steppingstone to getting to the higher levels of vibration. You don't want to go back down to the anxiety and depression stage. If you can just continue to channel your frustrations through fun, creative outlets. It doesn't even have to be creative; it can be such basic things.

If you're not into as much exercise as some then maybe you could find an art project. Drawing, painting, pottery. Whatever makes you feel good. If it's going to annoy you and maybe make you angry, then I would recommend finding something where after you say, "Wow, that was great." You get a buzz or a good vibe. A feeling of knowing that whatever you just did helped you enrich your day. You can move up from anger to frustration then from there you can move up again.

You move away from where you want to be if you're not listening to or recognizing your emotions. If you want to find your soul purpose/know yourself, what you love and what truly makes you happy then you need to follow the good feeling emotions which will bring clarity. The good feeling thoughts. The good feeling experiences.

I really enjoyed doing some courses from Caroline Cory who developed the omnium method to help people become aware of just how amazing we truly are. She also has made documentary films. omniumuniverse.com. She discusses that emotions are a very important phenomenon. We need to discern our emotions properly. You don't know what you're working on if you're not listening to your emotions.

They are experienced all day. We need to know the mechanics of the emotions. We base decisions on our emotions—on the way we feel. We need to understand how they come about. We are all a bit confused how to interpret our emotions because we don't grow up learning how to utilize them.

Emotions are a feeling deriving from one's circumstances, mood, or relationships with others.

Emotion is a complex psycho physiological experience of an individual state of mind as interacting with biochemical (internal) and environment (external) influences.

Physiological (Internal) + Environment (External) = Emotion

So an emotion can have two components. The emotion is subjective. The person interprets the meaning. As you observe an external stimulus, you trigger the chemicals in your brain. There is a range of emotions. We all feel emotions differently.

As you come in contact with an external stimulus, it's your individual interpretation. It's your perception. Identifying and expressing your emotion is confusing. We don't know how to feel the emotion.

Thought clusters

Photon light particles

Plasma (Charged Matter)

Subatomic particles (interaction - electricity)

Every time you're thinking, you're creating tiny little clusters around your brain. They are accumulating and floating around. You can get headaches when you don't release all of the thought clusters around your head. You accumulate so much electricity and it weighs down on you.

They become photon light energy. You need to identify them and send them out into the unified field.

Emotional Clusters

These are more chemical components that are rejected by the body and not processed by the body. Emotions have chemical components including nitrates, oxidized iron, sodium nitrates.

When you are expressing an emotion, you are sending out things like tiny clouds. These are a gas form of all the chemical components in your cells.

You are made of chemistry and electricity. You are also more than that. You have your soul, your consciousness, your higher guidance. You are walking around with all of this stuff that you can't see. You are releasing chemistry through your emotions. They are undigested, and they need to come out.

We are told it's ok for girls to cry but for boys not to. We are taught from a limited human perspective. There are so many different layers of emotions. We are far more complex than just a physical body. Emotions are unique to being human.

Can you imagine not having emotions? Do you think you would miss them?

You are in charge of your emotions. Everything is purposeful. Your emotions are an amazing tool. They are an intelligent system. You can use it and master it.

Be aware of where your emotions are coming from. How are they making you feel mentally and physically?

Your emotions have a very specific purpose and that is to guide you. We need to discern and articulate our emotions, but it can be very hard to actually articulate them.

Is "embraced" an emotion? No. An emotion could be joyful, blissful, peaceful. Beautiful is not an emotion. It feels like home is not an emotion. Your physical feeling can be expansion. You can't release things if you don't know what the emotion is. You don't know what to heal.

When we have an emotion, it pushes us to take action and make a decision. The emotion is guiding us to do something. It helps you make the proper decision if you understand your emotions. It allows you to take charge if you are understanding your emotions which is your guidance system.

If you are feeling appreciation then usually you are feeling good. Your emotions and how you feel matters. The action you take will depend on your own personal belief system. One person that is angry may take a completely different action than another. It's dependent on how you grew up and what you have learned. That doesn't define you, though. You can start fresh and be whoever you want to be.

Emotions have different frequencies. We can have a range of emotions at the same time. Every cell has a combination of emotions, for example contentment, fear, freedom, etc. and another could have a combination of guilt, happiness, and anger.

You are unique. Emotion is subjective. It depends on your interpretation. You are moving the emotion and handling the emotion. You are in charge of your emotions.

"You are the creator of the external experience not the other way around."
- Caroline Cory

Your emotions are your guidance to tell you how to deal with different situations. Emotions make you take action. Depending on what emotions you have depends on the actions you take. Emotions have learned behavior.

We assume that everyone reacts the same way to the environment, but it's not the case. You might be watching a movie about a couple being in love and you have a steady partner, so you think it's an uplifting, happy, beautiful movie. Your friend sitting next to you might have broken up with their partner and are feeling miserable, so this movie is depressing and makes them anxious. Someone else could be feeling angry because their partner cheated on them, so they just want to kick the tv. It's so subjective. You just don't know what anyone else is feeling. All you can do is focus on how you are feeling.

Emotion is a learned behavior. You learn to display emotion because of your belief system. It's supposed to be natural, but we have been shaped by others.

Our parents might have taught us that something is not acceptable. For example, if we were being really loud. We start to create blocks because we have been told that certain things aren't ok, and we are trying to please others.

You change the automatic structure, and you create an energy block. The emotional system is like a river. It comes in, it gets processed and then it goes out. But we can start to create blocks in our river. It can look like a block of ice, for example. So the ice doesn't flow through us as easily as a river of water.

An emotional block is stagnant energy. Stagnant information. If we are feeling clear, then everything flows and is continually being processed in an organic way. We aren't supposed to store anything, but that's what we end up doing. We get things stuck in our bodies.

We haven't been taught how to release blocks. We don't allow a natural flow of information. You force the flow into another form by pushing down your emotions. Experience what is happening. Allow the emotion to come to the surface. Recognize your emotions. Interpret your guidance's message.

You can then make a decision on what you want to create. We often block our feelings. Your emotions are a guidance system. So what is your reaction to something that happens that you're not happy with? Are you feeling frustrated, angry? Do you just want to go and eat unhealthy foods, or do you want to punch something?

Try and think, "I need the clarity for this emotion. Please bring clarity."

Deep in your heart cells you have a belief system from years ago. You can relieve the belief system. The root cause. You don't need to know the exact root cause. You often create particular situations in life so you can clear old blocks and belief systems. You will keep getting angry and annoyed. Similar situations will keep repeating themselves until you have cleared the blocks that are stuck in your body. That's why your emotions are a great tool. You don't want to overthink why you are angry. You want to release it and realize where it came from. Do you want to go back to eating unhealthy food and continue to be angry or have you processed it and allowed it to flow through you?

On a higher level you have created your reality. You can choose to create abundance without worrying about what everyone else is doing or what everyone else says. It doesn't matter what your neighbor is doing or what the government is doing. It's all up to you to enjoy and create, explore, and discover.

Instead of saying to a child, "Stop being angry, that's not acceptable behavior. You're bad, you're naughty!" You could say, "Tell me how you are feeling. Tell me what it's like to be angry."

Allow them to feel it.

"Do you understand feeling angry is natural? But you can do something with it. It's making you want to do something. You can use anger to do something positive and something that makes you feel good."

Teach them how to process it rather than blocking it and pushing it deeper. You can obviously do this to yourself. Don't be hard on yourself for having emotions. You can feel angry. Feel frustrated. It can be motivation to create and expand.

You don't need to feel your emotions and have a huge emotional response. That's when you start to overthink it and repeat old habits. All you need to do is ask yourself, "How am I feeling? I'm feeling angry about that annoying person. Why? My mum told me not to feel angry so I'm trying to block feeling angry."

All you need to do is find an easy way to release it. Negative energy is a toxin in your system. It's a fine line of not bringing up the past and triggering yourself but it's good to release past beliefs and behaviors.

If you're not manifesting something it's because that's not who you really are. Don't get frustrated if something you think you wanted hasn't happened because maybe that isn't your path. A job you think you really want might not be the right one because if you got this glamorous high paid job you might be completely stressed and overwhelmed and have no time for play.

What you're trying to create might not be your true essence. Make a decision about what you might want to create. Don't think about the job or a project. Think about what you really want. It doesn't have to be specific.

"I want to be happy."

"I want to have time to play."

"I want to have the money for freedom."

Create a reality that is fun and enjoyable. You hardly have to do anything. We are overthinking everything.

Our brain channels are an electrical signal. Everything we do sends an electrical signal out into the unified field. Make a decision. You want to create something that's in alignment with who you are. You just need to start with the basics. Your brain channels will align. You don't need the whole big picture. You don't even need the steps of where to start.

"I want something that is going to be in alignment with who I am." Keep focusing on basic things you want. Visualize having it. Happiness, abundance, wellness, excitement. Whatever makes you feel good. Just put it out there into the Universe.

You will start to get more clarity on what you want and what it will look like. The job ideas will start to come. The money will start to come. The relationships, the house. Just get in alignment. A place where you feel satisfied where you are.

Why do we have feelings? If you're not supposed to feel then what's the point of feelings? You can learn to feel your emotions and release them then move up to better feeling emotions.

We get used to not allowing feelings to come through. Think about ways you can release blocked emotions. Exercise, meditation, mindfulness, healing practitioners, music, yoga, Tai Chi, podcasts, laugh, sunlight, art, creative experiences, Feng Shui, healthy food, unplug from devices, rest, sleep, yoga nidra, crystals, nature, surfing, breathing techniques, pets and much more.

We are all here to create something different. It's up to you what works for you.

People have learned behaviors. Sometimes people have been brought up with violence, so they feel in order to fix something then violence is the right thing to do. This is what they have been taught. This is why I find it hard to condemn anyone because they believe they are doing the right thing. This is what they have grown up with. This is what they believe. This is a continuous cycle.

They see external things that show it's unfair. So they are teaching each other a lesson. They are trying to fix things but it's in a violent way. The learned behavior has been taught that violence is the way to fix things. You think people are cruel or heartless but it's their learned behavior. They think they are doing the right thing. They aren't processing their emotions properly. In some people's minds they have the logic that what they are doing is right. They need support and education.

You might not feel worthy of having abundance or having a great job. But you are. Everyone deserves their dreams to come true. You can be whoever you want to be. You can reinvent yourself.

You need to guide yourself by the way you feel. You don't want to remain in anger, you want to move through it and move up to joy. You don't want to feel judged and feel like you're not good enough. Don't let anyone define who you are. You can do your best to feel good. Reach for anything that can make you feel better. Make you feel satisfied. It's a great start then you will keep moving up from there.

All matter is merely energy condensed to a slow vibration. Some believe we are all one consciousness experiencing itself subjectively.

Life is only a dream, and we are the imagination of ourselves.

Pretending to feel good all of the time is fine, but it's not at the same vibrational level. So you can "fake it till you make it." You just have to make sure that you actually feel good inside, not just pretend you are fine on the outside. The Universe knows if you are faking it. Just because you say one thing doesn't mean it's true. The vibration you're putting out there makes it obvious. It's like playing a song on the radio and trying to tell someone it's a different song than what it is. The vibrations of that song in the sound waves are still that song.

Notice how you feel. Your vibrations are giving you feedback. How you are feeling is what you are putting out there. Like a magnet, you are drawing in things on a similar vibration so if you want good things to come you need to get on the vibration of feeling good. If you want money, you need to feel like you already have it. If you want happiness, you need to find things that make you happy.

People are struggling to feel good because they are trying to control their outer world. They are trying to control what their partner is saying or doing. They are trying to control the traffic. If it is out of your control, why bother trying? You are just wasting your precious energy. It is the most amazing feeling when you just let go and realize that it's ok to not try and control things. It's the biggest relief. You can breathe and relax knowing that everyone else has their own guidance system. They have their own journey. Polarity and contrast are happening out there, but you don't need to get so stressed trying to help or fix things or feel sad or feel angry. Putting that energy out there is not as fun as putting out positive energy.

You are the designer of your destiny. "Everything is working out for me." The power within is greater than the power in the world. We are unlimited beings. Your purpose is what you say it is. Inner happiness is the fuel for success. Find something that resonates with your heart. Follow excitement. Act when you are inspired.

Abraham Hicks talks about how we are living in a "vibrational Universe." We are "eternal beings" who have come to this "leading-edge planet" for expansion. The Universe is full of goodness and love. A lot of people have forgotten who they are and lose their "guidance system." Everyone has downloaded "belief systems." We are taught this is "good," this is "bad." People have been taught by teachers, parents, religious leaders, governments, etc., so it's not anyone's fault that we don't understand each other.

A lot of the world hasn't caught up with who they are. They don't realize they are vibrational beings. That's why they say hurtful things. They have just lost their way. But the contrast is good for us because through us learning what we like and what we don't like we are sending off "rockets of desire" and bringing more of what we want into our reality and after we leave this world, we have the most amazing compilation of everything we desire.

The law of attraction as I understand it is that what we are putting out there we are bringing into our reality. The more you focus on something the more you see it. I started focusing on things that made me feel good. All I see is how many amazingly creative people are out there. So many people more than ever are enjoying crystals, going back to natural healing, loving all the things that were considered weird or "woo woo" years ago. There's always going to be people that disagree, but we are kind of disagreeing with their beliefs in a way.

I know there is pure goodness out there. They say that thoughts stay in the Universe forever and people pick up on those "thought forms" so if you're feeling a certain way about something you will just see and hear everything about that subject. You can have positive or negative thought forms depending on what frequency you are tuning into. I want people to have the happiness they deserve. That's why I decided to write this book because so many amazing people have helped me.

I'm definitely not worried about the "afterlife" anymore. There's no hell. No one is bad. We have this opportunity to be on this incredible planet. The "afterlife" is a beautiful vibrational world but on this planet we get the added bonus of touching, smelling, tasting, and hearing through our physical senses. I'm enjoying all of these incredible moments we have.

I've found I can't control the outside world and I can't control what anyone thinks but I can control my thoughts and feelings and I'm choosing to feel good.

I believe we are here for fun, discovering ourselves, expansion and enjoyment. Expanding our consciousness. It would be a boring world if we all agreed, and all thought exactly the same things. We wouldn't evolve as much and have such a great expansion. We are creating a bigger, broader Universe with our contrast.

"*There's a flawed premise that the more you do the more you're worth. The better you feel the more you allow. You could not be more deserving*" - Abraham Hicks. (abrahamhicks.com)

What Vibration Are You On?

Vibrational frequencies are like radio waves. Line up your frequencies to where you want to be. Do you feel like sometimes your thoughts aren't your own? You get inspiration for an amazing idea that came out of nowhere? That's the Universe sending you blocks of thought and ideas. You're receiving information. You need to line up with what you want because if you're feeling angry, vulnerable, or upset then you can end up with other random blocks of thought that have been put out into the earth's energy field. You can feel other people's anxiety and stress. That's why you have to look after yourself. You cannot help anyone else if you're stuck in a cycle with other people's lower vibrations or frequencies.

Just remember that what you put out there you will get back. If you're putting out negativity, then you will get on the same vibration as others that are negative. It's cause and effect. For example, you will attract people that are on that same vibe. If you're rude, you'll attract rude people. If you're saying you don't have enough money, then you will attract the vibration of lack. The Universe has a beautiful flow giving us what we desire but if you're putting blocks on everything with your mood, frustration and feeling lack of then you won't fully be living and creating your ideal world.

You create your reality. The more you watch something or do something the more real it becomes. You talk about a certain subject, and it becomes your reality. Have you noticed what you talk about or what you think about? We are vibrational beings. Look at us under a microscope and we are atoms and what is inside the atoms? Energy. We see what we want to see through our perceptions. We hear words that we are told, we believe them, then they become our reality. Can you shift your vibration to stay in alignment with your true self and be the person you are really meant to be? You may be stuck in a cycle of unwanted vibrations.

It's not your fault. It happens to all of us, but you can get out of them. Every day you can catch those negative thoughts. You can focus on what makes you happy. Think about what *REALLY* makes you happy. Stop saying I can't do that. Or that will never happen. Stop getting caught up in other people's drama or the world's controversy. Your reality is what you focus on. You are not ignoring problems or not caring. Wanting to feel good should be your highest priority. The Universe would prefer you put out vibrations that are positive, uplifting, joyful, peaceful, loving. Why would you want to send out the vibrations of negativity, unworthiness, worry, stress, anger, frustration, doubt, sadness? Imagine if the whole world started putting out more positivity. It would be an awesome party. Let's start with ourselves. There's no better time than now. Love yourself and the Universe will feel the shift.

Don't take your life too seriously. Laughter can have health benefits. Laugh. Have fun. Don't focus upon lack. People believe they must work hard, struggle and put effort into everything. If you put less effort in then your life becomes effortless. Easier. Its flows. It's in the attitude. Insist on a feeling of ease. Get in sync with the law. It gives you what you offer vibrationally.

One of my favorite sayings from Abraham Hicks is "Find the path of least resistance, find the path of most allowance." If you have to make a decision, even if it's something you don't really want to do then think about what is going to be the easiest option. The path of least resistance is the path that is going to make your life a bit easier in the long run. Instead of fighting against something that you're not going to be able to control then just go down the easier path.

We Have Freedom.

We can choose whatever we want. We can choose to get hurt. We can choose for things to go wrong. The Universe gives us whatever we are asking for. Total freedom of choice. This is why "bad" things happen to such "good" people. However they are feeling. Whatever their thoughts are. That is what you are putting out there. If you're feeling vulnerable something can get stolen. If you're not feeling safe, you can pick up on other energies from people over time that have not felt safe. Giving you anxiety or fear. You have to care about how you feel!! If you're feeling a lack of money then you will have a lack of money. You know how so many rich people got that way? They just expect it. Expectation is everything. You can't just say, "I expect money to come in." You have to feel it. Feel abundance. Own it. It's like a deep knowing.

THE UNIVERSE DOESN'T USE WORDS: it speaks in vibration. Can you imagine the Universe speaking in all of the languages of all of the planets? No wonder people are saying it speaks as a vibrational language. One language for all. We've just forgotten how to speak in this vibrational language. The way you can start to remember is by getting in touch with your feelings. How you are feeling is the vibrational language you are putting out there. Like a magnet, you are getting back what you are putting out there. Cause and effect. Care about what you are thinking. Care about what you are saying. Care about how you are feeling.

For a while I've been wanting to understand something. So they say a lot of what we are doing is creating our own reality, then how do you know if you've caused something to happen or if it's your guidance telling you something is going to happen?

A podcast from Abraham Hicks explained it this way: If you are tuned in, you find yourself in a good mood, and things have been flowing, then if you receive the information that something might happen, it's probably more valuable information than if you're stressed out and angry, worried or sad.

When a thought comes up that is a bit unsettling there's usually a solution that's behind it. But it helps to be feeling good and tuned in. You just have to be ready and feeling good so that when things come to you, the solutions appear, and everything seems to flow more easily.

There's always an answer and a solution.

There is a vibrational reality that is there. You just have to keep practicing raising your vibration and feeling good. It definitely took me a while. I was trying way too hard to feel good.

It's like tuning into a radio station. Some days I still switch off and feel frustrated. So much fighting and controversy. People thanking others for going to war to kill other people. I just look at the world pretending that I'm observing from space, looking at the same species of humans fighting with each other and not getting along. But luckily now it doesn't take me long to realize that it's part of our journey. They are expanding the Universe with their wars and controversies. I can't change them, but I can help myself and feel so much better and enjoy life. It just starts with one. Imagine if we all just looked after ourselves and focused on what makes us happy instead of trying to make everyone else happy. It can be contagious, this happiness thing. Own where you are. Let it be alright. Then start finding things that make you feel good.

Words that you can use daily:

Sureness
Certainty
Knowing
Being
Love
Like me
Honest

DREAM

Deep
Soul
Source
Basic
Good
Soft
Gentle

Appreciate
Comfortable
Flows
Secure
Fun
Certain
Real

BELIEVE

DO WHAT YOU LOVE

Adoring
Expansion
Alive
Full
Grateful
Inspire

You may be thinking, well why haven't we all heard that you can create your own reality or heard about the law of attraction earlier? Wouldn't we have all been doing it by now? That's the thing—this "secret" has been here all along. They say so many great minds knew about it. Einstein,

Leonardo, it's just that it's hard to figure it all out completely. When there is so much overstimulation in the world and beliefs we've been taught we are not going to get drawn to this information. Over time it's being unraveled. If others or even you don't believe it, that's totally fine. Some days I find it hard to believe it myself. It sounds completely crazy when I read my words sometimes or listen to what I'm saying. All I know is that my life has become 111 percent better.

Some will say, "But if you create your own reality then wouldn't we all win the lotto?" There are so many factors that go with it. If it was that straightforward then yes we would all win the lotto. Firstly, how many of us truly believe that we would win the lotto? Secondly, sometimes in the back of our minds the thought of having a lot of money is actually stressful. Do you need to give some to family members, charity, do you feel worthy etc.? Thirdly, we have been told so many times that money doesn't grow on trees, and you can't just instantly get what you want. You have to work for your money. The resistance that's built up since birth has put a stop to a lot of our lotto winning dreams. What are the odds of us actually all winning lotto? Money can flow in other ways. Don't just expect it from lotto. Let the Universe surprise and delight you.

Just start with slowly finding thoughts and feelings that make you feel better over time and see what happens for yourself. Don't put pressure on yourself to win the lotto because you are actually doing the opposite to creating it.

Clear your mind. Think of what you desire and visualize yourself already having it. What does it look like? What does it feel like? What does it smell like? Keep practicing; you'll get there. I would believe that in some way the money or relationships are going to come. You don't have to know where from.

I know I could be completely crazy along with many others like me, but I don't really care. It feels so good that if I am crazy, then that's awesome. I remember when I first started I was manifesting butterflies. I said to the Universe, "RIGHT NOW, UNIVERSE, IF YOU'RE REAL

THEN YOU NEED TO PROVE IT TO ME." Then literally as I finished saying it a butterfly flew so fast above my head and hovered in front of me. I have never seen anything like it. I got chills down my spine. I was literally speechless. It was the most perfect timing. Obviously anyone could say it was just a coincidence and yes it could be but since then it's been happening more and more. Whatever is happening it's super fun and I am definitely not going to go back to how I was.

I had an amazing childhood, and my parents are the best, so I've been very lucky. I have always tried to stay positive, but this is a next level of expansion. It's like I was a cocoon for so long and now I've got my wings and I can fly.

You can become a vibrational match to your dreams.

CHAPTER 11

BRING ON THE GOOD VIBES

"Believe in your heart that you're meant to live a life full of passion, purpose, magic and miracles."

- ROY T. BENNETT

Sending love and good vibes!!! Don't waste your energy on things that are out of your control. You can't change anyone else's brain. It really helps to focus on yourself. Do what makes you happy. Focus on the good things around you. It can be very basic things. I find when I'm happy everyone else around me is positive and happier. Cause and effect. What you think about you get back. What you put out there you get back. Keep practicing by focusing on yourself and appreciating life. You deserve the best!! You're amazing.

Everyone wants to be loved.

Everyone wants to be happy.

Everyone wants to be joyful.

Everyone wants to be free.

Everyone wants to have fun.

Everyone wants to feel good.

You were born magnificent, and you still are magnificent. You were born to be happy and add value to yourself and others. Born to contribute to the expansion of all that is. With your focus, with your desires, with your wants and needs, you are expanding the Universe.

This contrast we are living in is creating more desires, more expansion, and more evolution. More creations are happening. More awakenings of the soul are being discovered. Out of the problems come the solutions. You are pure positive energy. You are loved, so worthy, valuable, beautiful and incredible. We are right where we are meant to be. Sending lots of love!!

I think we all want the same thing. We just go about it differently. Diversity helps us evolve and move forward. It helps us choose what we like and what we don't like.

You can't create reality while you're facing reality.

So many people are still holding onto the past. Wouldn't it be amazing if the whole world could do a total reset? A time where everyone let go of the angst of their old beliefs, of their resentment and their frustrations. I would never want to disrespect what anyone has gone through, but I feel that holding onto problems and blaming the past is exhausting and those blocks in your body cause illness, disease and ageing. You weren't born to suffer. You were born to explore, expand and evolve. You are expanding creation through everything that you are doing. Through the contrast, through what you are discovering that you like and don't like, you are expanding the Universe.

Energetically we are all connected. We are part of this earth, and we are part of one another.

What you resist persists. Your freedom is absolute. Contrast helps your expansion. You are here for freedom, growth, and joy. You came to find alignment with who you really are. It's a law-based universe. Everything you talk about you attract even if you say, "No, I don't want it." You still attract it. You are activating the frequency of it.

Healthy Mind/Body/Soul

I'm not a doctor, health professional, or expert. These are just things I've learned on my journey. I'm not saying they are right or wrong. It's up to you to decide if anything resonates with you. My goal is to help more people feel good. Intend for healing. You deserve to feel good and well.

You are a seed ready to blossom.

Have some self-love. Accept yourself as you are right now. Welcome imperfections by focusing on what you have gained from the process of doing the best you can. Avoid focusing on what you cannot do. Instead focus on what you can do.

Let go of the old and invite the new. Go beyond the mind and be who you are truly meant to be. You are stronger, more powerful, and incredible than you could ever possibly imagine. Stop living a limitless life and start creating a life that you deserve. There's enough for everyone.

There's a field of energy that connects all things. A pure positive energy.

There is a field of unbounded consciousness. A field of possibilities. There is a vibrational manifestation before we physically manifest but sometimes we are impatient or have beliefs that we are not deserving, or it will never happen.

"You need to be in a place where you are called to what you do really want." - Abraham Hicks

In other words, you need to have all areas aligned within yourself. You won't find the right job or the right relationship or more money until you know who you are. You know what you like from the contrast. From lessons learned of bad workplaces or bad relationships. All of those things have helped you get closer to what you really want. It all needs to start with you. You need to be happy first. We can right ourselves and so can the planet.

You are an ever evolving being so you're going to keep being inspired, keep manifesting dreams. Your purpose is going to evolve with you.

Don't try to make something more complicated. Figure out a rough idea about what you like, what you want, and visualize yourself already having it. The trick is you must believe it so if you don't believe you can have it then it might not come. Or it could take years to arrive. You need to make sure you don't have any blocks on the subject. Do you feel worthy? Do you worry that it's not fair if you get something when other people don't have things? Don't worry about that—there is plenty to go around for everyone.

This is why meditation is so powerful. You stop all the thoughts that are telling you that it's not possible or too hard. In meditation, you can stop all of the resistance so that what you really want can flow in.

Be patient. In the beginning, you feel like you're not getting anywhere. Over time it gets easier and better, then eventually it all clicks. Keep preserving by finding things that make you feel good. Care about feeling good or feeling better than you used to. Meditation calms the mind so you can hear your body telling you what it needs and wants. It helps with illness and injuries.

"I'm a vibrational being, living in a vibrational Universe. I'm here to come to my own personal conclusions about what I want. I'm here to launch rockets of desire. I know I'm not vibrationally up to speed with them yet, but I know that I can be, and I have a hunch that getting up to speed with them is the fun of life. I'm happy there are still things for me to be eager about, I'm going to give myself a break." - Abraham Hicks Spotify Podcast Quote

You are not disappointing the Universe. You don't have to be perfect. You are here to learn and grow, discover, and evolve. You don't have to put so much pressure on yourself to do everything, be everything, please everyone and please the Universe to get you into a good place for the "afterlife." You are a leading-edge creator here to enjoy the physical manifestation of things. What an amazing opportunity to have fun, play, laugh, create. You haven't been sent here because you have done something wrong. You are here for expansion, to see, touch, taste, laugh, feel, create in this physical world.

When you ask the Universe expands.

If you're ready for what you want, the Universe starts to bring it to you.

Don't give your power away hoping to be accepted by others. What are you focusing on? Are you focusing on the news? What's wrong with the world? What you're doing wrong? What you don't like? Whatever you are focusing on you are bringing more of it. Don't get stuck in the drama and the negativity. You can become addicted to it all. It's like an adrenaline buzz that gets you up and going but it's not healthy or fun to keep living in that way.

You have a pure positive energy space that is there waiting for you. You've connected to it many times, but the contrast and resistance keep you away sometimes. It's always there. Endlessly flowing.

Do you want to face reality, or do you want to create reality? You might say well how can I ignore what's right in front of me. Yes, it's there but don't you want to start creating a world for everyone where people are happier, more content and enjoying life? It all starts with you. We can't change other people's perceptions until we change our own. We can't inspire others to create a more loving, peaceful world until we look inside ourselves. Are you telling yourself kind words? You are so worthy and incredible.

We haven't come here to prove anything to anyone. We have come for expansion for evolution. To see what we can be.

"It's an old paradigm to think that we need to suffer and that there needs to be war. You need to choose to be the future human" - Caroline Cory.

"You are good
enough, smart
enough, beautiful
enough, strong
enough."
LollyDaskal

Care about How You Feel

The best way to attract positive energy is to vibrate higher by sending out positive energy each and every day with your thoughts, feelings, and actions. It may seem like a tall order, but when you get the hang of it, you'll love all of the good vibes. Once you start attracting positive energy, you'll do whatever it takes to raise your vibration and live at a high-vibrational frequency.

Imagine and feel your future self now. When you can imagine or feel what it would be like NOW to be successful, or have that amazing relationship, job, money whatever it is you want to happen in your life, you actually start aligning with that future self. That's the first step in manifesting.

Always tap into what you appreciate—all things big and small. Appreciation is one of the highest vibrational frequencies and the fastest way to attract more positive energy to you!

Tip: Think of three things you appreciate every day.

What excites you? What delights you? What makes you feel good? What makes you feel healthy? Forget everything you've seen on tv or in social media. What actually makes you feel good inside? Stop doing things that don't make you feel good. You are not here to endure, to suffer. You're not an unworthy person. You are absolutely incredible.

Get beyond the mind. Get rid of blocks and belief systems.

Through contrast, through personal experience, you'll find what you like and what you don't like. Each experience of contrast leads you closer to your desires.

You are goodness. You are pure positive energy. You are here as creators and architects of this physical reality. Everything you are doing is helping to expand the Universe. Even if you think it is small or insignificant, it is still helping us all to expand. Because of your asking, you are creating more solutions. Focus your attention on your heart. You are loved, so worthy, valuable, beautiful and incredible. Your thoughts are turning to things.

Living in the energy of love will always attract more positive energy to you and align you with the highest of frequencies. When you come from a place of love with all that you think and do, you attract high vibe people and situations into your life!

Try to be inspired. Do what makes you come alive and feeds your soul. The more you find what inspires you, the closer you will get to living the life of your dreams. Aligning with your purpose. When you're inspired and loving what you're doing, you're vibrating high, and the Universe will step in and align you with even more good.

Next time you're inspired then try to follow the energy and see where you end up. It's such a short-term gain to please others but so much more of a long-term gain to please yourself.

Don't be controlled by the information on the internet. Stop reacting to what you perceive is true. You pinch yourself off being jealous, frustrated, angry, and competitive. It's great if everyone else is successful. We all benefit.

The journey won't stay the end result because there will be another and another. Do everything in a state where you are focusing on the good aspects of your day. Try and find a way to enjoy what you're doing; put a positive spin on everything. Listen to uplifting podcasts or music that you love or try doing it meditatively. Try and look for the positive aspects in every situation.

Look at finding the present moment; that's where your power lies.

When you're fully present, aware of how you're feeling, then you can adjust how you're feeling. That's when you're attracting more positive energy. When you're present, you can make changes to align your thoughts and actions to a higher vibration.

be yourself

be passionate

find appreciation

judge less

send love

have fun

be happy

be satisfied

do what you love

POSITIVE
Affirmations

live in the now

feel abundant

be kind

be resilient

have compassion

be understanding

clear thoughts

be peaceful

dream big

be grateful

Awareness of Surroundings

Our skin and beliefs may be uniquely different, but our collective souls are the same. As one world we are so much stronger than standing alone. Fighting and war come from misunderstandings and frustrations. The belief systems leave us separated and divided. It is such a beautiful time to learn lessons and create a world of support, compassion, and love. We are all unique like different drops of the ocean. But in the end we are all connected as one ocean.

Wellness

Wellness is a proactive process that involves becoming aware of and making choices that contribute to a healthy and fulfilling life. It encompasses more than health; it is a dynamic process of change and growth. A favorable or satisfactory state of being is marked by health, happiness, prosperity, and wellbeing.

Wellness is the deliberate development of your entire self. Embarking on a wellness journey entails seeking out the appropriate "tools" to help you become a healthier and happier person and establishing your effective methods for utilizing these "tools" for continued growth and development. Due to the diversity inherent in all aspects of life, there are also an infinite number of ways to cultivate an ever-changing path of wellness. This definition is critical in two ways. First, wellness is not a static state, but an "active pursuit" defined by intentions, choices, and actions to pursue optimal health and wellbeing. Wellness is also connected to holistic health, which means that it encompasses more than physical health and has a variety of distinct dimensions that should work in harmony.

While wellness is an individual pursuit in which we are accountable for our own choices, behaviors, and lifestyles, it is also strongly influenced by the physical, social, and cultural environments in which we live. Aspects of your lifestyle are viewed as dimensions of overall wellness. They can include social connection, physical activity, nutrition, and mindfulness. These factors can affect your physical and mental wellbeing. By making simple and healthy daily choices, you can significantly reduce stress, foster positive social interactions, and achieve optimal wellness.

The term "wellness" is frequently used interchangeably with the terms "health," "wellbeing," and "happiness." While they share some characteristics, wellness differs because it does not refer to a fixed state of being (i.e., being happy, in good health, or a state of wellbeing). Rather, wellness is associated with an active process of awareness and decision-making that results in optimal holistic health and wellbeing.

Holism: Your health and well-being result from the continuous interaction of the various natural dimensions of life and wellness. Each dimension is intrinsically linked to the others. The goal is to be aware of yourself as a whole and complete person fully engaged in life.

Self-Responsibility: It's up to you to be in charge of health and happiness. You can't allow others to make decisions for you. You can get help but in the end no one can help if you don't help yourself. Self-responsibility is predicated on self-awareness, which is how an individual gradually becomes conscious of the potential impacts of their behavior.

Positive and Proactive: Wellness necessitates a predominance of positive perspectives and values. Additionally, it requires a strong sense of purpose and deliberate, conscious action. These are our underlying assumptions, which have stood the test of time. They do, however, provide a simple framework. What you choose to include within that framework is entirely up to you.

Balance: While acknowledging the ever-changing nature of your life, you strive to achieve balance by paying close attention to each dimension. Inadequate attention to any one dimension will result in less-than-optimal personal development and may even result in chronic unhappiness. Stress doesn't actually help me. Stress changes my cells, can mess with my immune system, age me, give me wrinkles. If it's out of my control, I can't do anything about it. Everyone has their own journey that they need to be a part of. You can use a daily mantra.

Mantra: "I am Strong x Happy x Healthy x Beautiful."

Types of wellness include:
Emotional Wellness

Emotional wellness is concerned with a person's self-image. This entails experiencing and expressing a range of emotions and developing the ability to manage those emotions rather than being controlled by them. While it is necessary to express all emotions, even if they include anger, jealousy, sadness, and so on, what is more critical is to act appropriately so that they serve you rather than harm you or someone close to you. By managing your emotions, you can increase your desire to participate in activities you enjoy, assist others with compassion, and foster more healthy relationships between you and others.

How to Optimize Your Emotional Well-Being:

Keep your body moving. Engage in some form of physical activity. Exercise. Household chores. (I love putting my Beats headphones on or earbuds and dancing around or listening to podcasts.) If the weather permits, venture outside. Circle the block. Run. The options are limitless. One of my favorites is Yoga for every aspect of life.

"Yoga for me is about getting back to your true authentic self. It takes away the layers you have accumulated since birth physically, emotionally and energetically. It helps guide you through your decision-making process and knowing what your next right step will be. It is a teacher a friend and true self love." *Jessemey Bank—Jasana.co Wellness & Living*

Develop a routine. Create a schedule that strikes a balance between the work you do and the life you desire. Establish a schedule for your meetings. Set aside time for yourself. Make space for what you enjoy.

Develop relationships with others. Maintain contact with those who support you. Those that are on the same vibe as you. You don't have to please everyone or hang out with people you don't want to, including family members. It's your life. Spend time with someone who inspires you.

Forgive. Allow others to forgive you and allow yourself to be forgiven. Forgiveness enables healing. Forgiveness paves the way for present-moment living. Forgiveness enables development and happiness.

Sleep. A restful night's sleep enables your body to heal. Sleep rejuvenates the brain, allowing it to manage memories and process information more efficiently. You awaken in a more positive mood. But don't think that you have to have eight hours. You can get up in the night, stay up or sleep in. The best thing about sleep is that it stops the momentum of the day if it's not going so well. Sleep allows us to reset and start fresh again.

Be gentle with yourself. What brings you happiness? Where do you feel most at ease? When will you have time to be yourself? As you practice self-kindness, you will want to extend that kindness to others.

Develop self-awareness. Take note of the thoughts, actions, habits, and personality traits that benefit you. And you'll be prepared when you identify what needs to change or adjust. You will intuitively know.

Social Wellness
Every day, individuals interact with one another. We can develop the ability to interact with others in a variety of settings and to resolve interpersonal conflicts peacefully when they arise. This sometimes entails hanging out with people that annoy us, but I just try not to let people get to me. I'm only hurting myself by being frustrated.

How to boost your social well-being:
• **Schedule it**
Make time to connect with others. Check-in with your family or friends when you feel like it. It's up to you to find what makes you feel good. Sometimes it's worth making the effort to check in.

- **Make it Personal**

While texting is frequently the default mode of communication these days, don't overlook the value of hearing and seeing one another. These audio and visual connections compel you to listen carefully and concentrate entirely on the person in front of you. As a result, you feel more personally heard and seen.

- **Build Transparency**

Relationships are formed through genuine, open communication. When you share your "true self," you develop a stronger sense of connection, love, and security in who you are and help others develop trust in themselves.

- **Take Responsibility**

When things go wrong, it's natural to point the finger at others. Relationships with coworkers, family, and friends can quickly deteriorate if you refuse to accept responsibility for a mistake or express regret when you have harmed a relationship. Be the first to apologize and, if necessary, seek restoration. If you find yourself falling short of your social connections, conduct a quick check-in to determine whether one of your relationships requires attention. This is a strategy for putting social wellness first.

- **Listen First**

Before expressing your opinion, listen to what others have to say. This is especially critical when discussing contentious issues where divergent views are likely. When your turn comes to speak, speak with humility. Rather than defending your position, approach the conversation with an open mind. Generally, being correct is less important than preserving the relationship.

Environmental Wellness

Environmental wellness is necessary for personal health to be optimal. This includes ensuring a safe food supply, reducing violence, preserving good air and water quality, and safeguarding ourselves against hazards.

How to Boost Your Environmental Wellness:

1. Establish a healthy, happy living environment

Determine the size of your personal living space. What is visually appealing, and what irritates you? Make a list of simple, concrete steps you can take to improve the look and feel of your space. For instance, you could eliminate clutter, add more color, or increase the amount of light coming in. Declutter for clarity,

2. Seek tranquility

Take a moment to appreciate your surroundings during your hectic day. This can be done anywhere, but it's even more special if done in a tranquil location. You can discover tranquility as you go about your daily activities. As you walk around, stop at a bench or space that appeals to you. Take a seat and focus on your breathing for a moment.

3. Promote harmonious relationships in your household

After a long day at school or work, you want to feel relaxed, at ease, and welcomed. The physical setting contributes only a portion of this sensation. Your interactions with the people affect your level of comfort and environmental wellness.

4. View your neighborhood as a tourist would.

Consider viewing your neighborhood, city, suburb with fresh eyes. What would you notice if you were on vacation? Which area of town would you like to visit as a tourist? This strengthens your sense of community and heightens your feelings of admiration and awe.

Intellectual Wellness

Intellectual well-being entails critical thinking, skill acquisition, and creativity. Individuals can improve their intellectual wellness by conversing with someone who has a different perspective or simply reading a book for pleasure. Having a breadth of knowledge across a range of subjects significantly impacts how we view ourselves, others, and the larger community.

Create

Possessing the ability to create benefits both your intellectual and mental health and as with reading, being creative has been shown to improve memory retention and emotional stability.

Spiritual Wellness

Spiritual well-being refers to notions such as a set of guiding beliefs, principles, or values that give life meaning and purpose, such as joy, love, compassion, and forgiveness. Spirituality enables us to acquire the inner serenity and peace required to navigate life's ups and downs. When we are "in touch" with this component of wellness, we can discover meaning in life events, consolation through difficult times, the beauty of life, the ability for compassion toward others, and personal purpose. This one is totally up to you. Believe what you want to believe. You may not want to believe any of it. That's your choice. xx

Investigate deeper meanings

Investigating deeper meanings and patterns in your life will help you realize that you control your destiny. Recognizing this can assist you in living a happy and healthy life.

Adopt a positive attitude

Eliminating negative thoughts will undoubtedly enrich your life. Allowing for the positive can provide you with the changes you desire for an extended time.

Happiness

Everyone in this world is attempting to find happiness in their unique way. Individuals have vastly different character traits, beliefs, religions, values, and ideals, but regardless of which path we take in life, we all want to end up somewhere where we can be happy. Because words are merely symbols, when I use the term "happy," I refer to an enduring joy that permeates your being daily. Happiness, to me, refers to a sense of inner peace, joy, bliss, and fulfillment. Happiness is a frame of consciousness defined by the positive and pleasurable influences and emotions encountered during your lifetime. Happiness is not a singular emotion, as contentment or joy are. It is more of a continuum that spans these two emotions.

A person who is content in life is not necessarily happy. Neither does a joyful person model guaranteed happiness. However, a happy person experiences both of these extremes of emotion. Happiness is a choice. A person who chooses to see the positive side of life and maintains a positive outlook is what we refer to as truly happy. Money, it is said, cannot buy happiness. However, as a friend once put it, "Money cannot buy happiness, but it also does not make me sad!"

When I refer to the "secret of happiness," I mean reaching a point in your life where happiness is your default state and is present in your being for the vast majority of the time. To discover the secret of happiness, we must first ask and answer a critical question. What precisely makes a person happy? Individuals have numerous ideas about what they desire in their lives to be happy. For some, financial abundance is the goal; for others, loving relationships are the goal; for many, a sense of fulfillment comes from helping others; for others, success in their chosen career is the goal; and for still others, freedom from oppression or persecution is the goal. A more balanced individual will determine that happiness comes from achieving a certain level of success and harmony in all of his significant areas of life, which is far easier said than done. While pursuing these goals may result in varying degrees of external happiness, are they truly the key to happiness?

Filling the void will not make you happy
I'd be content if I could land that new high-paying job. I'd be content if I could escape my small hometown. If I could only find the ideal partner, I

would be content. Many people have a single ideal goal that they believe will bring them the happiness they've been seeking. They perceive a certain void in their lives and remain unhappy until that void is filled. The sense of deficiency they carry in this area also contributes to their inability to fulfill it.

However, the realization is that even if you accomplish that one thing that you are certain will finally make you happy for the rest of your life, it will not significantly alter your circumstances. Sure, you'll experience temporary joy and excitement at finally accomplishing what you set out to do. Still, just as quickly as a fancy new car loses its once-exciting appeal, the happiness you gained from accomplishing the goal will fade or be replaced by new goals and desires that you'll be certain will finally make you happy once they're accomplished.

One of the reasons you can't find lasting happiness when you accomplish something is your remarkable ability to adapt to your life circumstances. When something is lacking in our lives, we believe that filling the void will provide us with the additional "thing" we require. However, once the void is filled, we adapt to our new situation, and the other thing becomes the new normal. Our problems or sources of unhappiness are always contextual. A homeless person who receives a sandwich from a stranger may experience the same or greater joy than a businessman who is treated to a five- course dinner. Because happiness is relative, it isn't easy to achieve lasting happiness by adding objects, people, or accomplishments to your life.

What if the preceding does not apply to you? Perhaps you have developed a practice of expressing gratitude for the things in your life and have discovered a way to remain grateful for everything you have without becoming so accustomed to them that they lose their appeal. Another underlying issue that jeopardizes your long-term happiness is the impermanence of life.

The impermanence of life

The world is in continuous evolution, and nothing is permanent or eternal. If your happiness is contingent upon your possessions, there is always the fear of losing them. If your happiness is contingent upon your physical appearance, you will eventually grow old and wrinkled. If your happiness is dependent on your friends, family, or partner, they will either pass, or we will be separated from them. There is always a way to lose or have taken away what makes you happy. The more we deny this and the harder we fight to keep the things we need, the more unhappy we will be when they are gone. This fact may appear depressing and grim, but this is only true if you believe that happiness must come from all of these external impermanent things. There is only one permanent thing, and it is the true source of lasting happiness. It may require some effort to locate, but it is completely free and always available to us.

Happiness comes from within

Can you be perfectly happy simply by taking a walk in nature? Can you sense tranquility while sitting alone in silence? Could you still feel pleased if you were stranded on a barren island? Everyone has a default emotional state. What do you feel when there are no external distractions, and your mind is clear of past or future thoughts? Is tranquility your default condition, or is it more negative, such as boredom, melancholy, or mild annoyance? I know that each of us possesses a profound sense of calm and joy, but often in life, we grow so distant from ourselves that we lose sight of it, and the inner serenity practically vanishes. We become so engrossed with external concerns that we lose sight of the internal. For many people, their minds never allow them to rest. Our heads' near-constant chatter hinders us from perceiving anything inwardly.

The secret to permanent happiness is learning to quiet our minds, go within, feel this profound joy, and then bring it out in our daily lives. The constant joy within is the only sort of happiness that cannot be taken or lost. Individuals who have developed the ability to feel good for no reason tap into this source, which is why they are happy while others with better life circumstances may not be. Your happiness is defined by who you truly are, by yourself. It bears no resemblance to your material belongings, relationships, accomplishments, or even to your physical body. Your pleasure is a natural state of being that exists in the inner recesses of your consciousness. You can ignore it and embrace the world's definition of happiness, but the things you cling to can quickly disappoint, disintegrate, fade, or even vanish from your life. Consider the following. Consider your inner state of happiness as a cake, with tangible goods, accomplishments, and connections serving as the frosting. While the icing adds significantly more to the cake, the cake itself is the true substance.

How to cultivate inner happiness

A critical step toward cultivating inner peace is to align the voice in your head with the happiness you desire. If your inner thoughts about the outer world are regularly negative, the negativity you generate will isolate you from your inner happiness. Develop the ability to manage your mind and interrupt your thoughts when you discover yourself thinking excessively negatively. Your mind is only a tool for your use, and it is critical to learn to control it so that it does not dominate you. Develop an optimistic mindset. It requires practice like with anything; you must repeat something often before it becomes a habit but breaking it will undoubtedly improve your life if you currently have a negative thought pattern. Practice seeing the best in people, the brighter side of things, and being appreciative for everything; eventually, thinking positively will be all that remains.

The ability to think positively about yourself is critical. Suppose the voice in your head is putting you down, telling you that you're not good enough, that you're incapable of accomplishing something, or simply that you're not a good person. In that case, you'll generate negativity within that suffocates your core positivity. The most critical step toward inner pleasure is learning to love yourself for who you are. Develop into the type of person you'd want to hang out with. As long as you are comfortable spending time alone, it will be easy to feel wonderful for no reason.

Why is happiness a choice?

How can you choose happiness if you have been harmed and are afflicted by circumstances beyond your control?

Each day, we have the option of happiness or misery. The difficulty is that we become trapped by our circumstances. We're having a difficult day at work. We've been in an accident, faced unexpected costs, and encountered other terrible situations. We do not take the big picture into account. We should be pleased with a place to live, transportation, and the ability to pay our expenses. Rather than that, our emotions fluctuate as a result of shifting circumstances. Many people prefer to blame their sadness on their circumstances. Yet, if happiness were just contingent on our circumstances, most people would rarely be happy, as no one lives without sorrow. We all encounter obstacles, setbacks, challenges, and disappointments. It is part of our human existence. While many people are educated and aware, many remain dissatisfied with their lives. Academically, they comprehend the paths to happiness, but knowledge without application is only education. We can study all of the factors that contribute to genuine, lasting pleasure, such as gratitude, forgiveness, love, and appreciation, but little will change unless and until we put them into practice regularly.

What you strive for, what you accomplish in life, is and will always be your destiny. The sensation is a deep-seated sense of fulfillment.

On the other hand, happiness results from a series of choices (consciously or unconsciously). There are several reasons why happiness enhances the enjoyment of life. Your level of happiness, or lack thereof, affects all of your daily encounters and interpersonal connections. If you're happy, you're much more likely to positively impact your partner, children, neighbors, friends, workplace, and community. When each of us is at our happiest, the world is a better place. Happiness is a choice. Each minute spent in anger or frustration results in a loss of sixty seconds of happiness. Sustain a state of contentment. Keep your integrity. Allow individuals to be themselves if they disagree. It is not important to please everyone in life. You already possess everything necessary for happiness.

It's not about what you say. It's how you feel. You can't say you're putting out good vibes and being frustrated at something. For fun try and say as many high-frequency words as you can. It only takes sixteen seconds to change your frequency. See if it makes a difference.

This planet is a magnificent playground for us to explore and enjoy. Now's your time to reconnect with the earth, yourself, and the people in your soul tribe. The Universe is reminding us to care about ourselves and others. Let's use our mindfulness skills and appreciate what we have and not what we don't have.

Stop and reset. Don't just go through the motions. Think of what's really important instead of living rushing, stressing, and not fully enjoying life. It's about the connection with the little things. You have to realize how amazing you truly are. Sending Good Vibes straight to you.

Life Is Meant to Be Fun

Have you ever stopped to think about the role models in your life? The teachers, the family members, the friends, social media, digital entertainment. Do you think you have picked up some habits from them over the years or are you truly your own person? We don't have to be defined by our past or be the person someone else wanted us to be. Now is your time to shine.

The Universe doesn't want bad things to happen to you, but you have to remember without darkness you wouldn't know what light is. Sometimes when we go through things, we really appreciate the other side. When you hit rock bottom, there's nowhere else to go but up.

There's a lot of people out there that have been through a lot. They get help which is awesome, but you have to keep in mind that the past has happened and there's no way of going back and changing it. You can try and get to the deeper root of a problem and try and unlock exactly what happened, but you are only keeping that issue activated. You can't ever get rid of it so instead of spending hours and hours reliving old trauma it is beneficial to focus on the now and what makes you happy. Completely change the subject of past experiences. You can still be triggered maybe by people or songs or movies but it's up to you if you want to continue to relive the past over and over again. Use it as your strength not your weakness.

Life can shape you and create someone that really knows what they want. A stronger powerful person. How can you create the future you want when you keep reliving the past? It's time to let go. Just remember when you're saying no to something then you're actually calling it towards you.

Why do you feel you need to work hard and suffer to get to where you want to be? Does that feel good? Does that seem right? Why would you endure life in order to feel good in the afterlife? That doesn't make sense. Life is for enjoyment.

Please know that it's not your fault. Things that have happened to you are because you've got caught up in the momentum. Try to live more for the future. We talk about living in the now but obviously if your now isn't fun then first try to find a better feeling place.

You can't expect your life to change if you are telling the same story. If you keep saying this happened to me and this happened to me. You just keep the same things coming back again and again and again and again! You are literally a different person than you were because your cells have regenerated.

Isn't it boring trying to please everyone else? Isn't it boring worrying that you're going to sound weird and different? We are the leading edge. We are in the contrast, and it actually makes us more inspired and more creative.

It's a journey so we are always doing maintenance on ourselves. We can't expect to be perfect and feel good and happy all of the time, but we can definitely feel better. It's like looking after a car. You still have to service it and make sure every area is ok. Same with our physical bodies, our mental bodies, and our energy bodies. I find it easier to get into a routine of having fun weekly, meditating, and finding enjoyable exercises.

Some say there are different levels of awakening. Different levels of awareness and understanding. You can reach a higher consciousness. Meaning your brain and body is more expanded. More aware. It allows more knowledge and energy to flow. This all may seem completely crazy to you. Over time things start to unfold more and you have a greater understanding about the Universe.

I'm sure I'll need to revise this book soon because we are evolving so fast these days there's another layer and level to all of this. My friend and I always say, "Don't overthink it all."

Life is supposed to fun. If we get too caught up in our beliefs and trying to figure it all out all day every day it's not as fun. What's exciting is when you try and find good, happiness, and satisfaction in your life and then new amazing avenues open up for you. Let the journey flow. Don't try and make too much happen. You end up pushing against the good stuff if you try too hard.

I have a passion to ensure that everyone can be their true selves. Be happy and appreciate our own gifts and idiosyncrasies. Imperfection is beauty, madness is genius, and it's better to be absolutely ridiculous than absolutely boring.

Thank you for being a part of my journey. It's time for you to create your own reality. Get out there and find your passions. Find what makes you happy. I hope you're able to find some peace and calm and a deeper understanding and awareness of how truly amazing you are. No one is wrong to believe in what they believe because it's their reality that they have created. It may not be what you want but that's their journey. Create your own.

The best thing you can do for yourself is to let go of things from the past. It's already happened, and we can't change it no matter how much we want to.

See yourself in a different way. Don't live for the "afterlife." It's a privilege to be here on earth.

The soul without imagination is like an observatory without a telescope.

It's like building a muscle. You keep working on it. A plane is off course over 95 percent of the time, but the pilot keeps adjusting and then it reaches its destination. Just have fun. Be yourself.

Thank you for being a part of my journey. It's time for you to create your own reality. Get out there and find your passions. Discover what makes you happy. I hope you're able to find some peace and calm and a deeper understanding and awareness of how truly amazing you are.

Thanks again.

Lots of love Indi B ♥ ♥ ♥

Follow our journey. We are all in this together.

@lilyleaf11 on Facebook, Instagram, Pinterest
Lilyleaf11.com

Review

If you enjoyed the book, I'd love it if you could please write a small review to support my little business. It all counts. Without you, the little businesses couldn't do it.

Thanks again. You are so amazing. Don't forget to join me and we can be on this journey together.

I would love to keep writing books so thanks for your review. It will really help!! Keep an eye open for my Journal and more books.

Xx Indi B♥

Follow @lilyleaf11 on Instagram, Facebook, Pinterest
Lilyleaf11.com

"The more you dream the more you are awake."

Indi B

Meditation Example

Welcome to a Lilyleaf guided meditation. Try and find a quiet space. If not, I find ear pods/headphones work well. Sit down in a comfortable position. I like to sit on a pillow and lean against the wall. I love sitting on a bean bag or I sit on the couch. You can sit outside or anywhere you like. I like to feel extra comfortable then I'm relaxed. None of this sitting perfectly. I'm not as disciplined as a monk. I do what makes me happy. Use blankets or more pillows. It's your practice. Do whatever works for you.

This practice is not meant to replace any medical advice. Please contact your medical provider/healthcare practitioners if you require more help. This meditation is intended for relaxation purposes only.

Well done for taking time for yourself. By doing this you are helping to send more positive energy to yourself, your family, friends, and the world. You are a truly amazing being. Sit comfortably. Take a deep breath. In for 1,2,3 and out for 4,5. 1,2,3,4,5. Breathe in again. In 1,2,3 and Out 1,2,3,4,5 In 1,2,3 Out 1,2,3,4,5. Just relax.

You have been born into the world to discover your dreams and desires. You are finding contrast every day, which helps you learn, discover, and expand your soul. You are a beautiful being who is pure positive energy. Breathe in... Breathe out... You have a beautiful connection to the Universe. Breathe in... Breathe out...

Some say that in the middle of the Universe where the pure positive energy comes from you can connect back to that energy. Your inner guidance system knows how. Just relax and let it take you there. Calm your thoughts. Watch them go by. Bring yourself back to pure positive energy. You have nothing to do right now. This time is just for you. Looking after yourself means you have more energy for your day. Breathe in... Breathe out. Visualize a beautiful glowing white light. This light is filled with pure positive energy. It is in the center of the Universe where there is pure love and goodness. The energy is flowing all around you. Swirling like a white light protection cocoon.

Breathe in... Breathe out... You are so relaxed and comfortable and safe. This beautiful white light has come from the middle of the Universe. On its way to you it flows through stars and brushes past planets. It is full of complete love. Breathe in... Breathe out... It hovers over the earth and connects with nature on its way. It flows through the fresh air from the tall trees. It flows through pure aqua rivers. It hugs the soft snow on the hills. It touches the warm sun and brings it directly to your face. It glows all around you with the strongest love you've ever felt. Breathe in... Breathe out.

Visualize this white light touching your skin. It sinks deep into your cells and heals them from the inside out. Scan your body to see which areas you would like to send some extra love and healing. Start with your head. Breathe in.... Breathe out... Send any pain or energies away that don't serve you. Move down to your neck then your shoulders. Breathe in... Breathe out... Focus on the white light healing any areas that are in need. Let it massage your back and shoulders... Visualize your cells healing and regenerating. Move down your chest and focus on the organs in your body. Each organ has cells that are communicating with each other and your body. Send them love. Don't overthink anything. Just let your body do the work. Your body knows what to do. Breathe in... Breathe out...

Now focus on one of the most magical parts of your body. Your heart. It has amazing power and intuition. Your heart is sending you pure love. Breathe in... Breathe out... Focus on your hips. The hips hold a lot of emotions. Let go of all the old memories, energies and feelings that don't serve you. The most important time is now. You don't need the past to control your future. You have the freedom to be whoever you want to be. Breathe in... Breathe out...

Focus on the white light that is still swirling around you with pure love and goodness. Its energy is sinking deep into your tissues and molecules and cells. Deep within your cells are atoms which are pure energy. The white light is penetrating this energy to make it stronger, healthier, and more powerful than it has ever been before. Breathe in…. Breathe out… Now focus on your digestive system. Send it lots of love.

Focus on your right arm... Now focus on your left arm. Send them both love. Focus on your reproductive system. Let the white light swirl around with pure positive energy. Focus on your left leg and foot and then focus on your right leg and foot. Set an intention of being happy, healthy and to enjoy life. Say, "I intend, to be more present, to enjoy the little moments in life. I intend to be complete wellness. I am beautiful and powerful. I deserve happiness."

Meditation from Lilyleaf11.com

"My Language"

Create your own language for your guides, angels, soul, inner being. Whatever you like to call it.

Some examples are

11:11 Means I'm protected, loved, and guided.

333 Slow down and take a break.

888 Money Money Money. It's coming!

222 Keep going, stay focused.

Purple means protection.

Butterflies means you're being guided.

Feathers mean your loved ones are with you.

You can make up anything you like but once you've finished, it's best to stick with those for a bit otherwise it could get confusing. You can tweak it. Just make your list on a day where you are feeling tuned in, feeling good. Take a few deep breaths and ask your guides to help you write it. You can write it over a few months or in a day. It's up to you. It's your language; you can do what you like.

"Do not let what you cannot do interfere with what you can do."

– *John Wooden*

Breathing Techniques

There are many ways available online to support your breathing. A popular one is "box breathing" that children in school and even Navy Seals use. It can relieve stress. It's taking slow deep breaths. It can help performance and concentration.

The slower you breathe out the more peace you have. Breathing is one of the most important things you can do. Children have more energy because they belly breathe. I highly recommend finding new breathing techniques.

I really enjoyed an article I read on breathing ideas from verywellmind. com

They have discussed some great techniques to help with breathing.

Alternate-Nostril Breathing

Alternate-nostril breathing (nadi sodhana). This involves blocking off one nostril at a time. You breathe in one nostril then through the other, alternating between nostrils in a regular pattern. It's best to practice this type of breathing in a seated position in order to maintain your posture.

1. Put your right hand by bending your pointer and middle fingers into your palm, leaving your thumb, ring finger, and pinky extended.
2. Close your eyes or softly gaze downward.
3. Inhale and exhale to begin.
4. Close off your right nostril.
5. Inhale through your left nostril.
6. Close off your left nostril with your ring finger.
7. Open and exhale through your right nostril.
8. Inhale through your right nostril.
9. Close off your right nostril.

10. Open and exhale through your left nostril.

11. Inhale through your left nostril.

If you begin to feel lightheaded, don't panic. This is normal. Keep going or just take a break if you need to. I think just use your intuition to guide you.

Belly Breathing

It is said that belly breathing each day can reduce anxiety and stress. Find a comfortable, quiet place to sit or lie down. Try sitting on a chair, sitting cross-legged, or lying on your back with a pillow under your knees.

1. Place one hand on your heart and the other hand on your belly.
2. Allow your belly to relax, without forcing it inward by squeezing or clenching your muscles.
3. Breathe in slowly through your nose. The air should move into your nose and downward so that you feel your stomach rise with your other hand and fall inward (toward your spine).
4. Exhale slowly through your nose again or your mouth. My yogi would say that the energy is released through the mouth. It's just for eating but listen to your intuition. Sometimes you can purge unwanted energies.

4-7-8 Breathing

The 4-7-8 breathing exercise, also called the relaxing breath, acts as a natural tranquilizer for the nervous system. At first, it's best to perform the exercise seated with your back straight. Once you become more familiar with the breathing exercise, however, you can perform it while lying in bed:

1. Place and keep the tip of your tongue against the ridge of tissue behind your upper front teeth for the duration of the exercise.
2. Completely exhale through your mouth, making a whoosh sound.
3. Close your mouth and inhale quietly through your nose to a mental count of four.

4. Hold your breath for a count of seven.

5. Exhale completely through your mouth, making a whoosh sound to a count of eight.

Lion's Breath

With lion's breath, (*simhasana* in Sanskrit), you stick out your tongue and roar like a lion. This is another helpful deep breathing practice. It can help relax the muscles in your face, jaw, alleviate stress, and improve cardiovascular functions.

You can do this standing or in a seated position, stand up or sit up straight. Bend your knees and roar!

1. Spread your fingers as wide as possible.

2. Inhale through your nose.

3. Open your mouth wide, stick out your tongue, and stretch it down toward your chin.

4. Exhale forcefully, carrying the breath across the root of your tongue.

5. While exhaling, make a "ha" sound that comes from deep within your abdomen.

6. Breathe normally for a few moments.

7. Repeat the lion's breath up to seven times.

Mindful Breathing

Mindfulness meditation involves focusing on your breathing and bringing your attention to the present without allowing your mind to drift off to the past or future.

1. Choose a calming focus, including a sound ("om"), positive word ("peace"), or phrase ("breathe in calm, breath out tension") to repeat silently as you inhale or exhale.

2. Let go and relax. When you notice your mind has drifted, take a deep breath and gently return your attention to the present.

Pursed-Lip Breathing

Pursed-lip breathing is a simple breathing technique that will help make deep breaths slower and more intentional. This technique has been found to benefit people who have anxiety associated with lung conditions like emphysema and chronic obstructive pulmonary disease.

1. Sit in a comfortable position, with your neck and shoulders relaxed.
2. Keeping your mouth closed, inhale slowly through your nostrils for two seconds.
3. Exhale through your mouth for four seconds, puckering your mouth as if giving a kiss.
4. Keep your breath slow and steady while breathing out.

To get the correct breathing pattern, experts recommend practicing pursed lip breathing four to five times a day.

Simple Breathing Exercise

You can perform this exercise as often as needed. It can be done standing up, sitting down, or lying down. If you find this exercise difficult or believe it's making you anxious or panicky, stop for now. Try it again in a day or so and build up the time gradually.

1. Inhale slowly and deeply through your nose. Keep your shoulders relaxed. Your abdomen should expand, and your chest should rise very little.
2. Exhale slowly through your mouth. As you blow air out, purse your lips slightly, but keep your jaw relaxed. You may hear a soft "whooshing" sound as you exhale.
3. Repeat this breathing exercise. Do it for several minutes until you start to feel better.

Breathing Techniques Inspired by

https://www.verywellmind.com/

Reference Page

Lilyleaf Boutique
https://lilyleaf11.com/

Lilyleaf11 Publishing Co.
https://lilyleaf11.com/

https://www.abraham-hicks.com/
Abraham-Hicks Publications - Law of Attraction Official Site

Visual Photography by:
Theodore Trimmer
Zolotarevs
VAndreas
jakkapan
Jacob Lund
Nadya Korobkova
www.shutterstock.com

https://www.ellenstudio.co
Graphic Design
Design by Leah Ellen Lim

https://drjoedispenza.com/
The Official Website of Dr Joe Dispenza

https://www.deepakchopra.com/
Deepak Chopra™ - Official Website

https://eckharttolle.com
Eckhart Tolle

https://www.greggbraden.com/
Gregg Braden Best-Selling Author bridging modern science & human potential.

https://www.brucelipton.com/
Bruce Lipton is an American developmental biologist notable for his views on epigenetics, cell biology.

https://www.facetimeclinic.co.nz/
Beauty & Wellness

https://elevatehealth.nz/
Elevate Health NZ – Welcome ~ Nau Mai

https://www.jasana.co/
Wellness & Living

https://oraaromatherapy.com/
Ordinary Rituals Aromatherapy

https://georgiaellahealth.com/
Homeopathy Wellness

http://reneeskitchen.co.nz/
Food & Wellbeing

https://www.ramdass.org/
Ram Dass

https://www.healthline.com
Chakra's, Health info and more

https://www.omniumuniverse.com/
Caroline Cory

https://www.superhumanfilm.com/
Caroline Cory

https://www.Bepure.co.nz
Supplements & Wellness

https://www.gaia.com/
https://www.spotify.com/nz/
https://www.apple.com/nz/apple-music/
https://www.newscientist.com/definition/quantum-physics/
Definitions

https://www.space.com/
StarDust

https://www.brainyquote.com/topics/crystal-quotes
Quotes

https://www.mindbodygreen.com
Aura

https://www.verywellmind.com/
Breathing Techniques

ABOUT INDI B + LILYLEAF11 PUBLISHING CO.

Indi B. has been researching and studying various ideas on her travels. Her journey started with a little online boutique store in Red Beach, New Zealand. She designs and creates while enjoying life. One of her greatest passions is helping people to reach their full potential. When she's not writing she loves doing yoga, meditation, body combat, dance and watching surfing. She loves researching things which make people feel good and helps people discover ways to find true happiness.

Want more information about her journeys? Visit lilyleaf11.com to join the mailing list and receive a free PDF on crystal properties and how to cleanse your crystals.

Lilyleaf11 Publishing Co. Is a boutique company that was designed to allow Lilyleaf to self-publish books to help others on their own journey through life. These have been personally written and developed by Lilyleaf. We just want people to enjoy life.

For more information/ Press Enquiries; please contact:
hello@lilyeaf11.com

Lilyleaf11.com

Inspiration

- ♥ Mum + Dad
- ♥ Taj + Ari + Wyn
- ♥ My beautiful family & friends
- ♥ Melissa Jade Facetime Skin Clinic
- ♥ Leah Ellen Design Studio
- ♥ Julia Elevate Health
- ♥ Jessemey Bank Jasana.co
- ♥ Georgia Ella Homeopathy
- ♥ Ema Frost
- ♥ Kate Ora Aromatherapy
- ♥ Renee Rigden
- ♥ Daphne Luke
- ♥ Abraham Hicks
- ♥ Goop
- ♥ Dr Joe Dispenza
- ♥ Emma Mildon
- ♥ Rachel Hunter
- ♥ Ripe Kitchen
- ♥ Deepak Chopra
- ♥ Aikam Aikoham Nath Ji
- ♥ Caroline Cory
- ♥ Kelly Smith Mindful in minutes
- ♥ The World
- ♥ The Universe

Other Interesting People & Topics

Abraham Hicks *Emotional Scale Guide*
Dr Joe Dispenza
Caroline Cory
Goop
Deepak Chopra
Gregg Braden
Bruce Lipton
String Theory
Double-slit experiment
Quantum Physics
Quantum Mechanics
Quantum Healing
Peter Crone *Mind Architect*
Lewis Howes *The School of Greatness*
Meditation
Mindfulness
Yoga
Tai Chi
Dimensions
Energy
Law of Vibration
Feng Shui
Ayurveda

Touch this page for Good Vibes
Sending You Love

Your Amazing
Love Indi B xxx

Made in the USA
Monee, IL
16 October 2022